Defense Industrial Base

Critical Infrastructure and Key Resources
Sector-Specific Plan as input to the
National Infrastructure Protection Plan

May 2007

Homeland
Security

Department
of Defense

Preface

In June 2006, the Secretary of Homeland Security, supported by the Secretary of Defense and all other Federal cabinet Heads, published the National Infrastructure Protection Plan (NIPP) as called for in the National Strategy for Homeland Security and Homeland Security Presidential Directive-7 *Critical Infrastructure Identification, Prioritization, and Protection*, December 17, 2003 (HSPD-7). The NIPP provides the overarching approach for integrating the Nation's many Critical Infrastructure and Key Resources protection initiatives into a single national effort.

Recognizing that each Critical Infrastructure sector possesses its own unique characteristics, operating models, and risk landscapes, HSPD-7 designates Federal Government Sector Specific Agencies (SSA) for each sector. The Department of Defense (DoD) is designated the SSA for the Defense Industrial Base (DIB).

The Department of Defense is pleased to publish this Sector Specific Plan for the DIB. This Plan is a product of extensive collaboration among DoD, its interagency partners, and representatives of the private sector. Our national and international private sector partners make up the majority of DIB owners/operators, and range from small proprietors to Fortune 500 corporations employing tens of thousands of people. It is only through their continued voluntary cooperation that the important work of protecting the defense industrial base can be achieved.

This Plan is a living document. As the national security environment continues to evolve, so must our plans. To this end, the DIB partners have committed to periodic Plan reviews and revisions ensuring the highest standard of preparedness and readiness of the DIB sector. The Defense Industrial Base is an unmatched element of National Power that differentiates the United States from all potential opponents. Protection of the DIB is paramount to maintain that competitive advantage in executing National Strategy.

Peter F. Verga
Acting Assistant Secretary of Defense for
Homeland Defense and Americas' Security Affairs

OFFICE OF THE ASSISTANT SECRETARY OF DEFENSE
2600 DEFENSE PENTAGON
WASHINGTON, DC 20301-2600

HOMELAND
DEFENSE

MEMORANDUM FOR ASSISTANT SECRETARY OF DEFENSE (HOMELAND
DEFENSE & AMERICAS' SECURITY AFFAIRS)

SUBJECT: Government Coordinating Council Approval of the Defense Industrial Base
Sector Specific Plan

The National Infrastructure Protection Plan (NIPP) provides the unifying structure for the integration of critical infrastructure and key resources (CI/KR) protection efforts into a single national program. The NIPP provides an overall framework for integrating programs and activities that are underway in the various sectors, as well as new and developing CI/KR protection efforts. The NIPP includes 17 sector-specific plans that detail the application of the overall risk management framework to each specific sector.

Each SSP describes a collaborative effort between the private sector; State, local, and tribal governments; nongovernmental organizations; and the Federal Government. This collaboration will result in the prioritization of protection initiatives and investments within and across sectors to ensure that resources can be applied where they contribute the most to risk mitigation by lowering vulnerabilities, deterring threats, and minimizing the consequences of attacks and other incidents. The Defense Industrial Base Government Coordinating Council commits to:

- Support SSP concepts and processes, and carry out assigned functional responsibilities regarding the protection of CI/KR as described herein;
- Work with the Department of Defense and the Secretary of Homeland Security, as appropriate and consistent with their own agency-specific authorities, resources, and programs, to coordinate funding and implementation of programs that enhance CI/KR protection.
- Cooperate and coordinate with the Department of Defense and the Secretary of Homeland Security, in accordance with guidance provided in HSPD-7, as appropriate and consistent with their own agency-specific authorities, resources, and programs, to facilitate CI/KR protection;
- Develop or modify existing interagency and agency-specific CI/KR plans, as appropriate, to facilitate compliance with the Defense Industrial Base Sector Specific Plan;
- Develop and maintain partnerships for CI/KR protection with appropriate State, regional, local, tribal, and international entities; the private sector; and nongovernmental organizations; and
- Protect critical infrastructure information according to the Protected Critical Infrastructure Information Program or other appropriate guidelines, and share CI/KR

protection-related information, as appropriate and consistent with their own agency-specific authorities and the process described herein.

William Bryan
Director, Defense Critical Infrastructure
Chairman, Government Coordinating
   Council

Defense Industrial Base Critical Infrastructure Protection
Sector Coordinating Council

December 27, 2006

Mr. Peter F. Verga
Acting Assistant Secretary of Defense for Homeland Defense
     and Americas' Security Affairs
2600 Defense Pentagon
Washington DC 20301-2600

Dear Mr. Verga:

On behalf of the Defense Industrial Base (DIB) Sector Coordinating Council (SCC) I hereby acknowledge your issuance of the Sector Specific Plan for the Defense Industrial Base in support of the National Infrastructure Protection Plan. While this document is most directly a product of the Department of Defense, acting in its governmental role as the Sector Specific Agency, the DIB SCC appreciates having had the opportunity to participate in the development and refinement of the Plan prior to your signature.

The DIB SCC is confident that the collaborative effort and partnership model described in the plan will foster the relationships necessary to facilitate and prioritize protection initiatives to ensure both public and private resources are applied where they offer the most benefit for mitigating risk.

On behalf of the DIB SCC, I acknowledge that we:

    Support SSP concepts and processes, and will work with the Department of Defense and other security partners to develop and implement the plan,

    Have had the opportunity to provide insights and guidance on the unique needs, concerns, and perspectives of our organizations and members,

    Will establish and maintain partnerships for CI/KR protection with appropriate Federal, State, regional, local, tribal, and international entities, other private sector entities, and nongovernmental organizations, and

    Will work with the Department of Defense and the Department of Homeland Security to find suitable mechanisms for sharing CI/KR protection-related information.

Sincerely,

Barry D. Bates
Major General, USA (Ret)
Chairman, DIB Sector Coordinating Council

Table of Contents

List of Tables

Executive Summary

This Defense Industrial Base (DIB) Sector-Specific Plan (SSP), developed in collaboration with industry and government security partners, provides sector-level critical infrastructure and key resources (CI/KR) protection guidance. The DIB SSP outlines the Department of Defense (DoD) approach to executing Sector-Specific Agency (SSA) responsibilities assigned by Homeland Security Presidential Directive 7 (HSPD-7), Critical Infrastructure Identification, Prioritization, and Protection, December 17, 2003, and follows the 2006 CI/KR Protection SSP Guidance established by the Department of Homeland Security (DHS). It complements other DoD critical infrastructure policy.

To ensure effective integration with the National Infrastructure Protection Plan (NIPP) Base Plan, the following sections are included:

1. Sector Profile and Goals

This section describes the DIB Sector and the taxonomy used to classify the DIB products and services. It identifies security partners in government and the private sector, and discusses their roles and responsibilities. The section includes the DIB Sector's goals and desired long-term security posture and provides a value proposition for security partners.

2. Identify Assets, Systems, Networks, and Functions

This section discusses the information parameters, requirements, and methodologies that DoD and the DIB owners/operators use to identify their assets, systems, networks, and critical functionality. The section focuses on the process to identify those assets, systems, networks, and functions that, if damaged, would result in unacceptable consequences to the DoD mission, national economic security, public health and safety, or public confidence.

3. Assess Risks

This section complements the NIPP risk management framework, the basis of the national protection strategy, and includes a description of the DIB risk assessment process. By focusing on risk, protection efforts and resources are applied to achieve the greatest benefit. Risk assessments include consequence, vulnerability, and threat analysis. DoD is evaluating the existing criteria for identifying critical assets to determine if it adequately assesses the impacts to the DoD mission, national economic security, public health and safety, and public confidence. Modifications to the assessment criteria will be developed and implemented if required.

4. Prioritize Infrastructure

This section describes the process for performing a risk-based prioritization of DIB assets, systems, networks, and functions included in the sector. The key element is an Asset Prioritization Model (APM) that includes 16 distinct factors broadly classified into Mission (5), Threat (5), Economic (4), and Other (2) categories.

5. Develop and Implement Protective Programs

The emphasis of this section is on discussion of a layered "defense in depth" approach to infrastructure protection. The approach relies on collaborative implementation of self-assessment and self-protection in the private sector, dependence on local emergency responders for the next level of protection, and direct action by the SSA in the most extreme circumstances or when the most critical assets are involved. Plans developed under this paradigm help manage risks by deterring threats, mitigating vulnerabilities, and/or minimizing the associated consequences.

6. Measure Progress

This section describes how the DIB Sector measures risk management success. It addresses the development of goals and associated metrics to continuously improve the DIB Sector's protection and risk mitigation efforts. This section will be refined as the sector's risk management process matures. The national goals and metrics will be integrated into this section when provided by the DHS.

7. CI/KR Protection Research and Development (R&D)

CI/KR Protection R&D specific to the DIB Sector is in its earliest stages. As the DIB risk management process matures, DoD will collect unmet requirements for meeting security goals. DoD will partner with the DHS to leverage existing programs, advocate for national solutions, or initiate sector-specific R&D efforts as appropriate. This section discusses the current state of the concepts, ideas, and mechanisms available, and projects a collaborative methodology for further development.

8. Managing and Coordinating SSA Responsibilities

Per HSPD-7, DoD is the SSA responsible for collaboration with the DIB security partners, conducting or facilitating DIB vulnerability assessments, and encouraging risk management strategies to protect and mitigate the effects of attacks. This section describes the management process developed by the SSA to support those responsibilities assigned by HSPD-7.

This plan, developed as an annex to the NIPP Base Plan, describes the initial efforts to enhance the protection of the DIB. The SSP will be reviewed annually to reflect improvements and to address changes to the threat, technology, and sector profile. Revisions will be coordinated with DIB sector security partners.

Introduction

The Department of Defense (DoD) is executing the Strategy for Homeland Defense and Civil Support that builds upon the concept of an active, layered defense called for in the National Defense Strategy. This active, layered defense is global, seamlessly integrating U.S. capabilities in the forward regions of the world, the global commons of space and cyber space, the geographic approaches to U.S. Territory, and within the United States itself. It is a defense in depth. Near the actual and figurative core of this defense lie the critical infrastructure and key resources (CI/KR) of the United States essential to the Nation's security, economic vitality, and way of life. CI/KR includes the assets, systems, networks, and functions that provide vital services to the Nation. Terrorist attacks on CI/KR and other manmade or natural disasters could disrupt the functioning of government and business alike, and produce cascading effects far beyond the affected infrastructure sector and physical location of the incident. Direct attacks could result in large-scale human casualties, property destruction, and economic damage, and could profoundly damage national prestige, morale, and confidence. Terrorist attacks that use components of the Nation's CI/KR as weapons of mass destruction could have even more devastating physical, psychological, and economic consequences.

Homeland Security Presidential Directive 7 (HSPD-7) assigns two distinct tasks to DoD. First, like all Federal departments and agencies, DoD is responsible for identifying, prioritizing, and protecting the infrastructure essential to its ongoing ability to execute its mission. Second, DoD is designated as the Sector-Specific Agency (SSA) charged with leading a collaborative, coordinated effort to identify, assess, and improve risk management of critical infrastructure within the Defense Industrial Base (DIB). Execution of these responsibilities fits very well within the framework of "Lead," "Support," and "Enable" construct articulated in the Strategy for Homeland Defense and Civil Support. In executing the HSPD-7 responsibility for its own assets, DoD is clearly in the Lead, and has published a directive covering the Defense Critical Infrastructure Program (DCIP), which includes DoD-owned elements of the DIB. Therefore, the efforts to identify, assess, and improve risk management of those DoD-owned assets are not addressed under this plan. Instead, this plan describes the collaborative environment where DoD can support and enable the efforts of other critical DIB asset owners/operators.

Building on the requirements of HSPD-7, the Secretary of Homeland Security, in coordination with the Secretary of Defense and the heads of all other Cabinet-level agencies, published the National Infrastructure Protection Plan (NIPP). The NIPP provides the framework for the unprecedented cooperation that is essential to develop, implement, and maintain a coordinated national effort that brings together government at all levels, the private sector, and international organizations and allies. An essential element of this framework is the complementary Sector-Specific Plans (SSP) required of each SSA. This document represents DoD's effort, as the SSA for the DIB, to prepare a plan that describes a vision and methodology to identify critical assets, assess risk, and improve risk management within the sector. DoD will lead industry partners in the few critical circumstances where it is appropriate, support civil authorities at the State and local levels who are the firstresponders to any incident at a DIB site, and enable all of our security partners to improve their own security preparedness.

This SSP supports the planning assumptions outlined in the NIPP and identifies DIB sector-specific planning assumptions relevant to protecting the sector's critical infrastructure. The remainder of this SSP is structured around each of the steps outlined in the risk management framework:

- **Set Security Goals**: Define specific outcomes, conditions, end points, or performance targets that collectively constitute an effective protective posture.

- **Identify Infrastructures**: Develop an inventory of the assets, systems, and networks, and the critical functions they provide, including infrastructure located outside the United States, that make up the Nation's critical infrastructure, and collect information pertinent to risk management.

- **Assess Risks**: Determine risk by combining potential direct and indirect consequences of a terrorist attack or other hazard (including dependencies and interdependencies associated with each identified asset, system, or network), known vulnerabilities to various potential hazards, and general or specific threat information.

- **Prioritize**: Aggregate and analyze assessment results to determine asset, system, and network criticality, and present a comprehensive picture of national infrastructure risk to establish protection priorities and provide the basis for protection planning and the informed allocation of resources.

- **Implement Protective Programs**: Select appropriate protective actions or programs to reduce the risk identified and secure the resources needed to address priorities.

- **Measure Effectiveness**: Use metrics and other evaluation procedures at the national and sector levels to measure progress and assess the effectiveness of the national infrastructure protection program.

The DIB is the Department of Defense, U.S. Government, and private sector worldwide industrial complex with capabilities to perform research and develop, produce, deliver, and maintain military weapon systems, sub-systems, components, or parts to meet military requirements necessary to fulfill the National Military Strategy (NMS). The DIB is comprised of hundreds of thousands of industrial sites. The preponderance of the DIB is privately owned and comprised of businesses of all sizes.

To execute the SSA responsibilities for the DIB successfully, DoD must initiate and maintain activities to build trust with the DIB critical asset owner/operators. This will support two-way information sharing and maintain meaningful relationships and frequent dialogue across the diverse array of DIB partners.

Private sector participation in executing the NIPP is voluntary. Many large defense industry firms place a great deal of emphasis on protecting their physical, human, and cyber assets. On the other hand, many of the medium and small size businesses are challenged to make the capital investments required to perform vulnerability assessments and build resiliency into their operational capabilities. This SSP lays out how DoD plans to work with DIB security partners to meet the intent of HSPD-7. Taken together, our efforts will build a safer, more secure, and resilient DIB by understanding and sharing information, building security partnerships, implementing long-term risk management programs, and maximizing efficient use of resources.

1. Sector Profile and Goals

1.1 Sector Profile

The DIB is DoD, the U.S. Government, and the private sector worldwide industrial complex with capabilities to perform research and development (R&D), design, produce, deliver, and maintain military weapon systems, subsystems, components, or parts to meet military requirements. The DIB includes hundreds of thousands of domestic and foreign entities and their subcontractors performing work for DoD and other Federal departments and agencies. Defense-related products and services provided by the DIB equip, inform, mobilize, deploy, and sustain forces conducting military operations worldwide.

The DIB does not include commercial infrastructure that provides, for example, power, communications, transportation, and other utilities that DoD warfighters and support organizations use to meet their respective operational needs. Those commercial infrastructures are addressed by the other SSAs and through dependency analysis.

Because only a small fraction of DIB facilities are DoD-owned, the efforts described in this document focus on DoD and government actions to support private owner/operator efforts at DIB facilities determined to be critical to national security. The Assistant Secretary of Defense for Homeland Defense & Americas' Security Affairs (ASD(HD&ASA)), working in coordination with all pertinent elements of DoD, will ensure the identification of critical DIB assets, facilitate risk assessment, and encourage remediation of privately owned critical-asset vulnerabilities. Roles and responsibilities within DoD for the DIB are discussed in more detail in later sections of this document.

Table 1-1: DIB Segments and Sub-segments

Segments	Sub-segments	Segments	Sub-segments
Missile	• Tactical Missile • Torpedo • Strategic Missile	Ammunition	• Bombs and Warheads • Cartridges & Fuses • Explosives
Aircraft	• Fixed Wing • Helicopter • Unmanned Aerial Vehical	Weapons	• Small • Medium • Large
Troop Support	• Soldier Systems • Clothing & Textile • Subsistence/Medical • Smoke Obscurant • Nuclear, Biological, Chemical Systems	Information Technology	• Command, Control, Computers, and Intelligence • Information Security • Trainers & Simulators • Computer Peripherals
Space	• Launch Vehicle • Satellite	Shipbuilding	• Surface Ship • Subsurface
Combat Vehicle	• Tracked Vehicle • Tactical Vehicle	Electronics	• Electronic Warfare • SONAR • RADAR

Table 1-2: Defense Industrial Base Commodities

Mechanical		
• Diesel Engines	• Automotive Transmission	• Nuclear Components
• Rocket Engines	• Landing Gear	• Hydraulics
• Turbine Engines	• Bearings	
• Aircraft Transmission	• Pumps & Compressors	

Structural		
• Forgings	• Depleted Uranium Armor	• Composites
• Castings	• Ceramic Armor	• Precious Metals

Electrical		
• Electrical Motors	• Auxiliary Power Units	• Aircraft Circuit Breakers
• Batteries Thermal	• Low Smoke Wire & Cable	• Switch Gear

Electronics		
• Optics	• Digitization	• Traveling Wave Tubes
• Guidance/Control	• GPS Receiver	• Circuit Boards
• Communication	• Semiconductors	• Software

The DIB is subdivided into Segments, Sub-segments, and Commodities that produce weapon system platforms, components, and expendables. This taxonomy is used throughout DoD to classify the contributions of particular DIB assets, as well as to analyze the criticality using subject matter experts from each of the areas. This categorization is most applicable to the analysis of impact on DoD mission accomplishment, but it may also contribute to the economic, life, and health consequence areas. As discussed in later sections, security partners throughout the DIB might organize analysis and response efforts around this taxonomy.

1.2 Security Partners

1.2.1 Within Department of Defense

HSPD-7 assigns the responsibility for collaborating with relevant partners, encouraging or conducting vulnerability assessments, and encouraging risk management practices for DIB CI/KR to the Secretary of Defense (SECDEF). Effectively executing these responsibilities requires a complex communications network of organizations with diverse roles and missions.

Assistant Secretary of Defense for Homeland Defense & Americas' Security Affairs (ASD(HD&ASA))

ASD(HD&ASA) is responsible for coordinating the protection of the department's critical infrastructure and for DoD participation in the Critical Infrastructure Protection (CIP) programs at the national, State, and local-levels. Also, commensurate with responsibilities assigned to DoD by HSPD-7, ASD(HD&ASA) serves SECDEF as the lead SSA official for the DIB.

ASD(HD&ASA) assigned responsibility for the Defense Critical Infrastructure Program (DCIP), including DIB SSA responsibilities, to the Director for CIP under the Deputy Assistant Secretary of Defense for Force Planning and Employment. The Director for CIP provides policy, program oversight, integration, and coordination of CIP activities through the DCIP, and leverages related DoD and national programs supporting CIP.

Undersecretary of Defense for Acquisition, Technology, and Logistics (USD(AT&L))

USD(AT&L) is the Principal Staff Assistant and advisor to SECDEF for all matters relating to the Defense Acquisition System. In addition, USD(AT&L) is the lead for developing industrial and technology base assessments of, and establishing policies to maintain, the capability of the DIB to meet DoD needs—a responsibility that overlaps heavily with DIB SSA responsibilities. Because of this overlap, USD(AT&L) has a primary role and contributes to the execution of DIB SSA responsibilities.

Defense Contract Management Agency (DCMA)

ASD(HD&ASA) has assigned DCMA as the operational lead for executing SSA responsibilities because of its established working relationship with DIB owners/operators. DCMA responsibilities are to plan and coordinate with all DoD Components and private sector partners that own or operate elements of the DIB to identify, analyze, and assess DIB critical assets and related impacts.

Assistant Secretary of Defense for Networks and Information Integration (ASD(NII))

ASD(NII) serves as the primary advisor to SECDEF for information assurance (IA), networks and network-centric policies and concepts, and DoD enterprise-wide architectures and information technology (IT). ASD(NII) works in consultation and coordination with the Under Secretary of Defense (Intelligence) (USD(I)), ASD(HD&ASA), and USD(AT&L) on IA and cyber-related policies and issues.

ASD(NII) is responsible for formulating and implementing enterprise-level defense strategies from the information, IT, and network-centric perspectives, including assuring the availability of the Global Information Grid (GIG). ASD(NII) must develop and maintain the DoD IA Program and assorted policies, procedures, and standards, and perform the duties and fulfill the responsibilities associated with information security. While ASD(NII) is responsible within DoD for assuring the availability of the GIG, those responsibilities do not extend to the private sector portion of the DIB. There is no specific cyber asset characterized as part of the DIB Sector. Individual DIB assets likely have cyber elements within them, but they are the responsibility of the asset owner/operator. Cyber security is part of the critical asset risk assessment process, and the expertise of ASD(NII) will be sought for development and distribution of best practices to be shared with all DIB security partners.

Undersecretary of Defense (Intelligence) (USD(I))

In accordance with DoD policy, USD(I) is the DoD Senior Security Official. Responsibilities include integration of risk-managed security and protection policies and programs for personnel, physical, industrial, information, operations, chemical/biological and DoD special access program security as well as research and technology protection.

Undersecretary of Defense (Personnel and Readiness) (USD(P&R))

USD(P&R) is the principal advisor to SECDEF regarding oversight and measurement of readiness to ensure forces can execute the National Military Strategy (NMS). The staff of P&R is overseeing development and implementation of the Defense Readiness Reporting System. When fully implemented, the system will integrate information regarding the elements of the DIB. This integration will permit a clear assessment of the DIB's ability, at any particular time, to deliver required assets to DoD to support mission execution.

1.2.2 Private Sector Owner/Operators and Organizations

DoD relies on private industry organizations to exchange information on DIB infrastructure. DoD partners with defense industry associations, such as the National Defense Industrial Association (NDIA), Aerospace Industries Association (AIA), National Classification Management Society (NCMS), American Society of Industrial Security (ASIS) International, and Industrial Security Working Group (ISWG) to identify issues and potential solutions. These and other defense industry associations make up the membership of the Sector Coordinating Council (SCC) described later in this document. Working with industry, DoD will develop protocols for sharing and protecting information about critical DIB assets with sector security partners.

1.2.3 Other Federal Departments and Agencies

DoD collaborates with representatives from the Department of Homeland Security (DHS), other SSAs, and appropriate supporting Federal departments and agencies to ensure that DIB SSP efforts are consistent with, and fully support, national CIP efforts and DoD national defense requirements.

The supporting roles of other Federal departments and agencies for the DIB include:

- **DHS, Office of Infrastructure Protection (OIP):**

  – Oversee the consistent use of SSA plan guidance across Federal departments and agencies;

  – Collaborate with DoD to deter, prevent, and defeat physical and cyber incidents perpetrated against the DIB;

  – Collaborate with DoD to conduct or facilitate vulnerability assessments of the DIB;

  – Coordinate development of risk management strategies to protect against and mitigate the effects of attacks against the DIB; and

  – Collaborate with DoD to identify and establish additional DIB-coordinating mechanisms that identify, prioritize, and coordinate protection of CI/KR; and facilitate sharing of information about physical and cyber threats, vulnerabilities, incidents, potential protective measures, and best practices.

- **DHS, Office of Cyber Security and Telecommunications (CST)**, together with OIP, is responsible for deterring, preventing, and defeating cyber incidents across all CI/KR sectors.

- **Federal Bureau of Investigation (FBI):**

  – Maintain awareness of critical DIB assets;

  – Ensure that the respective critical DIB asset owner/operator receives at least one face-to-face contact annually with the assigned Special Agent in Charge;

  – Investigate reported suspicious activity and provide feedback to the reporting official; and

  – Respond to incidents as required by the asset owner/operator or by State and local law enforcement officials.

- **Department of Energy (DOE):** Through the National Nuclear Security Administration (NNSA), DOE works to enhance national security through the military application of nuclear energy and by reducing the global threat from terrorism and weapons of mass destruction.

  NNSA has three goals regarding national security:

  – Nuclear Weapons Stewardship: Ensure that U.S. nuclear weapons continue to serve their essential deterrence role by maintaining and enhancing the safety, security, and reliability of the U.S. nuclear weapons stockpile;

  – Nuclear Nonproliferation: Provide technical leadership to limit or prevent the spread of materials, technology, and expertise relating to weapons of mass destruction; advance the technologies to detect the proliferation of weapons of mass destruction worldwide; and eliminate or secure inventories of surplus materials and infrastructure usable for nuclear weapons; and

  – Naval Reactors: Provide the U.S. Navy with safe, militarily effective nuclear propulsion plants and ensure their continued safe and reliable operation.

- **Department of Commerce (DOC):** Through the Bureau of Industry and Security (BIS), DOC advances U.S. national security, foreign policy, and economic objectives by ensuring an effective export control and treaty compliance system and promoting continued U.S. strategic technology and DIB leadership. BIS administers the Defense Priorities and Allocations System regulation (15 Code of Federal Regulations (CFR) Part 700) to require preferential acceptance and performance of contracts and orders for materials, services, and facilities needed to support approved national defense programs, including CIP and restoration. BIS also conducts primary research and analysis of critical technologies and industrial capabilities of key defense-related sectors using detailed surveys to provide essential financial and production data. These activities are authorized under the authority of the Defense Production Act of 1950, as amended, and Executive Order 12656. DOC's National Telecommunications and Information Administration carries out the primary mission-essential function—to "achieve robust communications capability for the Industrial/Commercial Sector"—directly supporting national essential functions and the DOC's role relating to the economic security component of CIP and homeland security, as mentioned in HSPD-7. Among DOC's CIP responsibilities is ensuring the U.S. commercial and industrial sectors acquire diverse communications capabilities.

- **Department of the Treasury**: The Secretary of the Treasury chairs the Committee on Foreign Investment in the United States (CFIUS) and provides the committee secretariat within the Office of the Assistant Secretary for International Affairs. DoD, along with 11 other Federal departments and agencies, participates in the committee to support the President in exercising his authority to suspend or prohibit any foreign acquisition, merger, or takeover of a U.S. corporation that is determined to threaten the national security of the United States.

- **Department of State (DOS)**:
  - Supports the efforts of DoD, foreign nations, and international organizations to strengthen protection of critical DIB assets located outside the United States;
  - Facilitates exchange of information between host nations, overseas DIB critical asset owners, and DoD;
  - Supports the U.S. ability to safeguard national security and further foreign policy objectives by controlling the export and temporary import of defense articles and services covered by the United States Munitions List.

- **White House Office of Science and Technology Policy (OSTP)**:
  - Coordinates interagency R&D to enhance protection of critical infrastructure; and
  - Helps identify research requirements and technologies that are applicable to the DIB and shares information on those technologies with DoD and the DIB.

1.2.4 State and Local Agencies

To coordinate the government role for protection of the DIB, DoD works with State and local authorities principally through Memoranda of Understanding (MOU) facilitated by the National Guard. This relationship ensures the incorporation of critical DIB assets and their supporting infrastructure (e.g., telecommunications, road or rail, energy, cyber networks) into local law enforcement and other emergency response planning. The emergency plans will address prioritization of response and other services; the level of resources required to meet emergency needs; monitoring of the assets under their cognizance in the local environment; and advice, assistance, and warning of impending threats and hazards.

DoD designation of a DIB asset as critical may result in significant insurance and liability considerations. Accordingly, DoD seeks to avoid public disclosure of the fact that a specific facility is a critical DIB asset. At this time, DoD will only advise State and local agencies that it has a significant interest in a facility and has requested that the facility receive enhanced consideration in their planning and services. Any involved party must coordinate the release of such information through DoD to avoid redundant or undesirable consequences. Sharing of sensitive and proprietary information requires the prior specific, informed approval of the asset owner, and recipients of any information will be required to keep DoD fully informed of the use and consequences of the information. Where appropriate, DoD will seek to protect information under the Final Rule for the Protection of Critical Infrastructure Information issued September 1, 2006.

1.2.5 International Organizations and Foreign Countries

Transnational business partnerships are common, so critical DIB assets may be located outside the United States. As part of its Homeland Defense and Civil Support strategy, DoD is working to improve international capabilities by working with other Federal departments and agencies, foreign governments, and international organizations. Sharing technology, capabilities, and expertise strengthens the Nation's ability to respond to threats and domestic emergencies. DoD seeks to leverage the expertise of international partners to improve its own capabilities in counterterrorism, maritime interception, and other missions critical to an active, layered defense.

Partnerships particularly relevant to the DIB include:

- **North American Technology Industrial Base Organization (NATIBO)**. Formally chartered in 1987 by DoD and the Canadian Department of National Defence (DND-Canada), NATIBO is committed to coordinating North American technology industrial base activities by promoting a cost-effective, healthy technology and industrial base that is responsive to the national and economic security needs of the United States and Canada. NATIBO's primary purpose is to identify and analyze key industrial sectors that are critical to defense, assess the viability of these sectors, identify issues and barriers related to viability, and develop strategies to enhance and sustain the health of the marketplace. The goals of the partnership are to:

  - Improve the defense posture of the North American technology and industrial base;
  - Reduce redundant efforts through bilateral cooperation on studies and projects relating to the defense technology and industrial base of the United States and Canada; and
  - Ensure that North American technology and industrial base considerations are taken into account during U.S. or Canadian military and/or civilian emergency planning activities.

- **DND-Canada**. Its roles in DIB CIP are to:

  - Work through a DoD/DND Steering Committee and Working Group to assist the two countries in obtaining a comprehensive DIB awareness, thereby providing a framework to enhance bilateral security and obtain mission assurance;
  - Assist in strategizing the establishment of a Canadian Defense Industrial Base Program to include critical infrastructure similar to the ASD(HD&ASA) DCIP;
  - Collaborate on a common Critical Asset List; and
  - Define requirements for a bi-national protection program.

- Security and Prosperity Partnership (SPP) for North America. The governments of the United States, Canada, and Mexico are launching the next generation of their common security strategy to further secure North America and ensure the streamlined movement of legitimate travelers and cargo across our shared borders. To this end, the three governments will work together to ensure the highest continent-wide security standards and streamlined risk-based border processes are achieved. Relevant to the DIB, this will include:

  - Developing and implementing a strategy to enhance North American maritime transportation and port security;
  - Enhancing partnerships on intelligence related to North American security; and
  - Developing and implementing a common approach to CIP and response to cross-border terrorist incidents and, as applicable, natural disasters.

Vision Statement for the Defense Industrial Base Sector

Ensure the ability of the DIB to support DoD missions and eliminate unacceptable risk to national security through informed infrastructure risk-management decisions.

1.3 Sector Security Goals

1.3.1 Elements and Characteristics of Sector Security Goals

The following is a candidate set of sector security goals that form the basis for discussion between the Government Coordinating Council (GCC) and the SCC. (The GCC and SCC are described later in this document.) The candidate set of security goals will be refined as additional risk assessment information is developed.

Critical Asset Reduction Goal: Sector resiliency will be most assured if no particular asset can be assessed as more critical than any other. While the ultimate ideal goal would be zero critical DIB assets, the sector will strive to reduce the number of critical assets whenever and wherever possible within fiscal and legal constraints. Sound risk management practices, including asset resiliency, mitigation of risks, and redundancy will be shared and advanced throughout the sector.

Personnel Security Goal: Ensure all personnel directly associated with a critical DIB asset are vetted for employment suitability, reliability, and trustworthiness using established processes commensurate with requirements of the respective positions held, in conformance with pertinent security policy.

Physical Security Goal: Determine the impact or consequence of critical DIB asset loss to the DoD mission(s) supported, the known or perceived threat, and the susceptibility to exploitation of vulnerabilities the threat is capable of perpetrating; identify specific DIB assets the destruction or disruption of which could result in human casualties or economic disruption similar to the effects of weapons of mass destruction; compile a composite of facility physical security risk assessments.

Information Security Goal: All information that identifies or otherwise describes characteristics of a critical DIB asset that is created, held, and maintained by the government or the private sector will be protected from unauthorized disclosure according to established procedures appropriate to the particular level of information.

Information Assurance Goal: DIB asset owners/operators will have functional and adequate plans in place for exercising prudent information assurance methods to protect the DIB asset, to control processes over the production or provisioning of the product or service, and to protect the product or service delivery systems, including the supply chain.

Insider Threat Goal: DoD will provide security education and training aids to DIB asset owners/operators not having a security program so that they may implement provisions for the vetting of system and network administrators commensurate with the consequences of the loss of sensitive or classified information, production or provisioning capability, and supply chain integrity.

Monitoring and Reporting Goal: Determine the effectiveness of government threat reporting to officials, owners, and operators responsible for critical DIB assets, and to local law enforcement officials and other first-responders including, as appropriate, the medical and mass transportation communities.

Training and Education Goal: Develop specific security education and training materials for critical DIB asset owner/operators.

1.3.2 Process to Establish Sector Security Goals

DoD collaborates with industry through the SCC to formulate achievable security goals that conform to the Federal Acquisition Regulations, the Defense Federal Acquisition Regulations, and other relevant DoD policy. Specific sector security goals will respond to validated requirements for improved security using the integrated risk management approach.

1.4 Value Proposition

DoD seeks a consensus-driven sector security construct that draws on the active, voluntary, and full engagement of all security partners, particularly private sector owner/operators. DoD can achieve this only if all participants recognize the business value of their participation. Three key areas of value are:

• Minimizing service disruption ensures consistent, predictable revenue flow;

• Resiliency and the ability to restore disrupted service provides a competitive advantage; and

• Public recognition for preparedness, continuity of service, and good corporate citizenship enhance corporate reputations with investors, customers, and potential employees.

Because the DIB contributes to the DoD ability to execute the U.S. National Security Strategy and the National Military Strategy, potential threats from adversaries always exist. The importance of DIB contributions to accomplishing critical national responsibilities makes security partners' full and visible engagement an important goal for DoD. Through their engagement, partners will obtain improved access to information regarding vulnerabilities and threats, as well as risk assessment and risk-reduction best practices. This information will provide a worthy return on investment in the form of continuity in a stressed environment, capability to respond to customer requirements, and good will with DoD and other customers.

2. Identify Assets, Systems, Networks, and Functions

The DIB is an extraordinarily large, diverse, complex, interdependent, independent, hierarchical, and free-flowing collection of asset owner/operators governed by varying regulations, laws, treaties, and precedents. DoD and DOC estimate that the DIB is composed of hundreds of thousands of worldwide government and private sector sites, with capabilities to perform R&D, design, production, delivery, and maintenance of military weapon systems, subsystems, components, and parts to meet military requirements.

Unlike other infrastructure sectors, the DIB is defined not based primarily on the type of goods and services it produces, but rather on who the customer is for these goods and services. It includes companies performing under direct contract with DoD, their subcontractors, and companies providing incidental materials and services to either. It ranges across all sectors and sub-sectors of the industrial landscape, includes services as well as products, and varies from one-person or family-owned businesses to the largest corporations in the world.

Because the DIB is defined by who the customer is and not what is produced, DIB assets may also belong to other infrastructure sectors. DoD works with the DHS and the other sector SSAs to identify overlaps and gaps in responsibility.

2.1 Defining Information Parameters

DoD collects the following information on potential critical DIB assets:

- Contractor and Government Entity code, name of company, street address, city, State;

- Contractor subject matter expert, facility security officers, and their contact information;

- Sales, employment, capacity utilization, square footage;

- Products, functions, production rates;

- Programs, components, and subsystems;

- Prime contractor or subcontractor;

- Critical subcontractors (first and second tier, selection criteria, products, and services);

- Business overview (e.g., privately or publicly held, non-U.S. owned);

- Financial information; and

- Critical technologies.

Once an asset is determined to be critical according to criteria discussed in section 3, DoD collects the following additional information:

- Longitude and latitude;

- Buildings or other structures where industry manufactures or stores critical items;

- Dependencies (services and support an asset requires to function):

  - Dependencies a sector's asset has on other assets in the same sector; and

  - Dependencies between assets from different sectors;

- Continuity and redundancy, including backups built into the asset (alternative sources of supply and backup production facilities);

- Impact on sector in cases of loss or failure (e.g., economic, public health and welfare, public psyche, national security);

- Existing protective actions (e.g., fencing, biometrics, firewalls); and

- Exposure to known foreign intelligence threat such as treaty compliance regimes.

2.2 Collecting Infrastructure Information

In addition to site surveys and visits, DoD collects data by various methods, including questionnaires, public sources (e.g., Dun & Bradstreet and other Internet information sources), and examining proprietary, nondisclosure, and purchasing agreements. DoD also cooperates with DOC/BIS in initiating targeted data collection of specific defense-related industries and critical technologies using BIS's mandatory data collection authorities.

DoD collects data annually from DIB assets to support the Industrial, Technology Capability and Financial/Economic Assessment Process. Data will also be collected during the Assurance Assessment Process and as required to support non-routine requests.

Currently, there are no regulatory requirements for DIB assets to provide infrastructure data. DIB assets provide data on a voluntary basis with assurances by DoD that measures and procedures are in place and will be followed to protect business-sensitive and proprietary information.

Asset information resides in electronic asset portfolios on a classified portal. The electronic asset portfolio is a documentation repository containing summaries of supporting documentation on DIB assets deemed critical. ASD(HD&ASA) and other DoD decision-makers use this information for risk management and continuity of operation purposes. Documents in the portfolio include:

- General Information;

- Industrial, Technology Capability, and Financial/Economic Assessments;

- Industrial Base Studies;

- Visit Reports;

- Vulnerability Assessment Results;

- Sector Characterization;

- Threat Assessments;

- Self-Assessments;

- Continuity Plans;

- Site Risk Assessments;

- Antiterrorism/Force Protection Education and Training Material;

- Asset-Supplied Briefings; and

- Other Assessment Results.

As appropriate, DoD will provide asset information to the DHS for inclusion in the National Asset Database.

2.3 Verifying Infrastructure Information

DoD periodically reviews all DIB asset data for accuracy and currency, consulting with asset owner/operators to verify the data. When information is incomplete or inaccurate, DoD collects additional information through follow-up site visits or telephone interviews.

Critical asset data may be classified due to the obvious implications for national security of releasing the information. Critical data is classified, handled, and disseminated according to the DoD CIP Security Classification Guide dated January 2003. Information classified as secret is transmitted via the Secret Internet Protocol Router Network (SIPRNET).

2.4 Updating Infrastructure Information

DoD continues to refine the methodology to consistently identify and prioritize critical assets. DoD reviews the Critical Asset List annually and vets the list through numerous organizations for review and validation.

3. Assess Risk

3.1 Use of Risk Assessment in the Sector

DIB assets are, with few exceptions, owned and operated by the private sector. Currently, there are no regulatory requirements for conducting formal risk assessments. Larger companies often include some level of risk assessment as part of prudent business practices. Working with its sector security partners, DoD aims to ensure awareness and use of risk management best practices throughout the DIB at all levels.

DoD has an aggressive program aimed at assessing the components of risk to critical DIB assets. Prior to the issuance of HSPD-7 and current NIPP guidance, DoD's DIB program focused on assessing and mitigating risk to DIB assets critical to accomplishing DoD missions. DoD is currently in the process of evaluating its practices and procedures to determine if they are adequate to accommodate the NIPP's broader focus and emphasis to areas other than government capability. Modifications to the practices and procedures will be developed and implemented if required.

When assessing DIB assets, DoD evaluates individual facilities rather than entire companies because a single company may own both critical and non-critical DIB assets. While cyber security is an issue that could affect any facility, DoD does not perform network- or system-level assessments. The DIB is best characterized as a loose confederation of assets where impacts of loss or damage tend to be discrete, so higher level analyses would not add value.

The risk assessment process for critical DIB assets provides an evaluation of factors that may cause the direct, indirect, temporary, or permanent loss or degradation of critical materials and services. The evaluation includes the following:

- Industrial and business analysis that defines the business, economic, technology, and production risks that may adversely affect the capacity of the supplier to provide the critical material or service;

- Common commercial infrastructure analysis that maps critical supplier dependencies and interdependencies with the supporting commercial infrastructure sources (e.g., energy, telecommunications, transportation) to identify potential single or otherwise significant points of failure, possible remediation actions, and resolution, where viable, through the responsible Federal departments and agencies;

- Predictive analysis processes that help to define or suggest the existence of a problem for a critical supplier before it would otherwise be known;

- Vulnerability assessments that define the vulnerabilities of the supplier, identify impact if lost, propose and rank countermeasures, and include a variety of assessment means and tools for use by the facility and the government, including a self-assessment process for early identification, evaluation, and resolution of mission-impacting issues; and

- Threat assessments for the full threat spectrum, from manmade threats including the actions of nation states, national and transnational criminal entities, and terrorists, to accidents and acts of nature.

3.2 Screening Infrastructure

Due to the large number of DIB assets, the voluntary nature of private sector compliance, and the limited resources available to carry out comprehensive risk assessments, DoD must perform an initial screening based on consequences of loss. The NIPP, based on criteria set forth in HSPD-7, tasks SSAs to consider four categories of consequences:

- **Human Impact**: Effect on human life and physical well-being (e.g., fatalities, injuries);

- **Economic Impact**: Direct and indirect effects on the economy (e.g., cost to rebuild the asset, costs to respond to and recover from attack, downstream costs resulting from the disruption of products or services, and long-term costs due to environmental damage);

- **Impact on Public Confidence**: Effect on public morale and confidence in national economic and political institutions; or

- **Impact on Government Capability**: Effect on the government's ability to maintain order, deliver minimum essential public services, ensure public health and safety, and carry out national security-related missions.

Based on pre-September 11, 2001, national security concerns, DoD's legacy DIB programs have focused on the last category. As DoD moves forward in response to HSPD-7 and the NIPP, it will evaluate its existing criteria for identifying critical assets to determine if they adequately assess the impacts to the DoD mission, national economic security, public health and safety, and public confidence. Modifications to the assessment criteria will be developed and implemented if required. At present, DoD considers three of the four criteria in prioritizing assets once they are on the Critical Asset List. This is described in section 4.

3.2.1 Mission-Oriented Screening

DoD first screens DIB assets to select those that are "important" to performing DoD missions. DIB facilities are considered Important if they satisfy any of the following criteria:

- They are a sole source;

- They use obsolete enabling/emerging technology;

- They require a long lead time;

- They lack surge production; and

- They have a significant unit cost escalation.

Additional criteria described in section 3.3 below are applied to important assets to determine which assets are "critical."

3.2.2 Human, Economic, and Public Confidence Impacts

DoD is in the process of evaluating whether its screening process and practices adequately address the impacts to potential human, economic, and symbolic consequences. The potential for large-scale public health and human safety incidents, the presence of hazardous materials, and local and national economic effects will be considered. Screening criteria may be guided by the following representative questions:

- Would destruction of the facility result in significant loss of life at or near the facility?

- Does the facility contain specialized material or equipment that, if destroyed, could cause a public health incident?

- Would destruction or impairment of the facility cause significant reduction in the gross domestic product?

- Does the facility house material necessary to maintain national economic stability?

- Does the facility house specialized material or equipment necessary to the continued viability of the national economy?

- Would destruction or impairment of the facility cause a significant impact on a particular economic sector?

3.3 Assessing Consequences

From the list of important assets described in section 3.2.1, DIB assets are then determined to be critical to the DoD mission if they satisfy any of the following criteria:

- They are a prime or subcontractor single source with unique technology or industrial capability that could significantly impact war fighter operations due to non-availability of materiel;

- They are a prime contractor with capabilities that support numerous programs or industries;

- They are a single source subcontractor with a long re-qualification time that supports numerous programs across the services; or

- They are an essential advanced technology source.

The list of mission-critical assets is reviewed, updated, and approved on an annual basis or as required by war-fighting operations. This process is currently fully internal to DoD. However, as the DIB Sector security partnership matures, the process for determining critical assets will be expanded to include input from other security partners as appropriate.

3.4 Assessing Vulnerabilities

Vulnerability assessments are done on many levels. DoD has instituted a process to provide Awareness Training to DIB asset owner/operators. The purpose of the Awareness Training is to provide DIB company personnel with information about the place of their asset within the overall DoD mission requirements and acquisition process so they will understand their roles and importance to the NMS at the corporate and site levels. The training focuses on:

- Protection of DoD interests;

- Protection of Federal interests;

- Mission assurance to the war fighters; and

- Importance of facilities fostering relationships with local responders and Federal, State, and local law enforcement/civil authorities for business recovery planning.

The Awareness Training also informs the asset owner/operators of the protection measures applied to their proprietary and business-sensitive information provided to DoD, as well as an overview of the DoD information-sharing responsibilities and procedures regarding this data.

Once critical DIB assets are identified and prioritized, the next step is to conduct standardized assessments. DoD, working through DCMA and the National Guard Bureau, has established a standardized mission assurance assessment for application to critical DIB assets. These assessments consider impact, vulnerability, and threat/hazard (whether from natural disaster, technological failure, human error, criminal activity, or terrorist attack). This approach to risk assessment ensures consideration of relevant factors for each DIB asset and a relative prioritization of risks to support military operations. National Guard Mission Assurance Assessment teams have been designated to conduct assessments of DIB assets in the United States.

3.5 Assessing Threats

DoD considers the full spectrum of threats, from natural disasters to intentional acts of the Nation's adversaries.

DoD will work closely with the DHS to share threat and hazard information on critical infrastructure. The DHS Office of Intelligence and Analysis incorporates intelligence and information from multiple sources to identify and assess threats. The Departments should also share baseline infrastructure asset information, including current status of infrastructure services and anomalous activities. Working closely with the DHS will also ensure proper integration of information from the U.S. Coast Guard (USCG), Transportation Security Administration (TSA), Immigration and Customs Enforcement, Customs and Border Protection, and other vital threat information sources.

The DHS also maintains a fusion center for threat and hazard information, the Homeland Infrastructure Threat and Risk Analysis Center (HITRAC). HITRAC evaluates and monitors current threats to U.S. infrastructure. The center also maintains situational awareness of infrastructure sectors and develops long-term strategic assessments of their risks by integrating threat information with the unique vulnerabilities and consequences of each sector.

The NIPP outlines a national CI/KR protection strategy that includes an information-sharing strategy. The NIPP emphasizes the need for a shift from a "strictly hierarchical to a networked model, allowing distribution and access to information both vertically and horizontally, as well as the ability to enable decentralized decision making." The NIPP information-sharing network will enable CIP security partners to share information (through both push and pull methods) and perform analyses.

DoD, in concert with the Office of the Director of National Intelligence (ODNI), will capitalize on appropriate defense and national intelligence assets to develop, support, and sustain an assessment of threats to the DIB. The National Military Command Center (NMCC), Defense Joint Intelligence Operations Center (DJIOC), and associated Combatant Commands Joint Intelligence Operations Centers, will coordinate with the DHS watch centers—the National Operations Center, National Infrastructure Coordination Center, National Communications Center, and U.S. Computer Emergency Readiness Team—to maintain awareness of, and respond to, threats to the DIB. Furthermore, DoD, through NMCC and DJIOC, will work with other standing and ad hoc watch centers such as those established by the FBI, Department of Justice, and the Secret Service during National Special Security Events. DJIOC coordinates the tasking of DoD assets and will work through ODNI to task national intelligence assets.

DoD's Counterintelligence Field Activity (CIFA) established the CIP Arrayed Threats System (CCATS) as the DIB Sector's primary method for obtaining threat-related information. This system leverages elements of the Defense Indications and Warning System and graphically depicts threat levels related to the DIB. CIFA provides reports on incidents or events at all DoD and DIB assets.

4. Prioritize Infrastructure

Because resources are limited, DoD and its DIB security partners seek to invest in assessment and remediation activities in the most effective manner possible. To that end, DoD prioritizes critical DIB assets on the basis of the potential impact if the asset is lost or degraded.

4.1 Asset Prioritization Model

DoD uses the APM to rank DIB assets for both analysis and reduction of risk. The APM is an index model whereby a higher score indicates a greater impact if the asset is lost. DoD prioritizes assets for additional assessment and vulnerability mitigation investment based on the resulting impact score. The impact score is also referred to as the asset's "criticality." The APM is a method to support scheduling decisions, not a substitute for more rigorous assessments such as vulnerability assessments or CIP Mission Assurance Assessments.

4.2 Asset Prioritization Factors

DoD calculates the APM score based on 16 distinct factors broadly classified into 4 categories: Mission (5 factors), Threat (5 factors), Economic (4 factors), and Other (2 factors). All the metrics use a 1 to 3 scale (1 being least critical, 3 being most critical) to evaluate each factor. Each factor's score is multiplied by a weighting factor ranging from 1 to16 and the products are combined. DoD bases the weighting factors on overall impact of loss to the DoD mission and on current and future economic considerations. The resulting numeric score (136 to 408) ranks DIB assets based on criticality.

Table 4-1: Prioritization Factors

Model Factor	Weighting	Factor Classification
Impact Multiple Programs	16	Mission
Impact Current War-Fighting Capabilities	15	Mission
Impact Projected War-Fighting Capabilities (e.g., OPLAN 5020)	14	Mission
Corporate Financial Risk[1]	13	Economic
Site Economic Viability[2]	12	Economic
Recovery Plan	11	Mission
Reconstitution – Time	10	Mission
Reconstitution – Cost	9	Economic
Threat – Known External Threats to Facility	8	Threat
Known Security Issues	7	Threat
Disaster Risk – Metric	6	Threat
Chem/Bio/Rad/Nuclear/Explosive Collateral Damage	5	Threat
Populated Area	4	Threat
Site Employment as Percentage of County or Metropolitan Statistical Area	3	Economic
DCIP Awareness Visit Followup	2	Other
Vulnerability Assessment or CIP Mission Assurance Assessment (Completed/Scheduled)	1	Other

4.3 Asset Prioritization Review and Update Process

DoD reviews and updates the APM methodology and data sources regularly, focusing on:

• Customer requirements and concerns;

• High-level guidance and policy;

• New information and sources that affect the model;

• New information technology and other process improvements; and

• Evolving risk picture throughout the sector.

DoD analysts calculate the APM scores in a secure computing environment and provide a final ranking of assets on the Critical Asset List. Once scores have been checked and verified, ASD(HD&ASA) determines the assessment schedule and remediation activities.

[1] Based on DCMA Industrial Analysis Center assessments.
[2] Based on DCMA's Economic Viability Assessment Model.

5. Implement Protective Programs

Absolute protection of all assets is neither technically nor financially feasible. Therefore, DIB asset owner/operators must have a way to prioritize protection investments. Risk management is integral to this. DoD encourages DIB asset owner/operators to apply a risk management approach to protecting DIB infrastructure. DoD assists owner/operators with understanding the risk—impact of loss, vulnerabilities, and threat—associated with a specific asset. When owner/operators deem risk unacceptable, they must take action to reduce risk by affecting at least one of the risk factors until risk is at an acceptable level. The owner/operators will select specific action(s) to reduce risk within the constraints of affordability and practicality.

Some risk-reduction actions may have negligible cost, such as procedural or operational changes. DoD encourages DIB asset owner/operators to implement the low-cost risk-reduction actions by making them aware of the benefits of such actions on business continuity. Other actions, such as implementation of proven and readily available security equipment and redundancy options, may be relatively low cost and easily handled within existing budgets. However, in some cases, risk reduction may require long-term planning, significant investment by the asset owner, a DoD resource commitment, or all of them.

DoD collaborates with DIB asset owner/operators to develop plans to implement protection recommendations based on the results of risk assessments. Remediation (correcting vulnerabilities), deterring threats (making an asset a less attractive target), and mitigation plans (managing the effects of the loss of an asset) are methods to reduce or eliminate the risk to an asset. Owner/operators make risk-reduction decisions, but DoD strives to facilitate informed decisions by encouraging information sharing and making decision-support tools available.

5.1 Overview of Sector Protective Program

The following protection principles of layered defense apply to DIB critical assets:

- **First level of protection**: Asset owners are responsible for the first level of protection. In addition to any inherent responsibility, such as an obligation to shareholders or creditors, there are contractual obligations or, in the case of facilities involving classified information, regulatory and legal standards that require basic levels of protection.

- **Second level of protection**: As the seriousness of threats escalate, local authorities will assist the asset owner in meeting protective responsibilities.

- **Third level of protection**: If the response from local authorities does not provide the necessary level of protection, State or Federal law enforcement authorities can be brought in to augment the protection measures.

- **Fourth level of protection**: In more serious situations, a State Governor may request other Federal assistance or employ the National Guard under his or her command and control to enhance protection.

- **Fifth level of protection**: When warranted, the President may direct the employment of U.S. military forces to protect threatened DIB assets.

The protection measures discussed in this section focus on facilitating relationships and sharing information to implement the appropriate level of protection as described above.

DoD will support all DIB asset owner/operators in their pursuit to reduce risk from an attack or hazard. DoD will share techniques and tools to make risk reduction easier for owner/operators. Also, when appropriate, DoD will collaborate with the owner/operators to jointly determine and take steps necessary to reduce risk.

For critical DIB assets, DoD will collaborate with owner/operators and appropriate Federal, State, and local authorities to prepare coordinated plans of action to prevent, deter, and mitigate the adverse effects of terrorist attacks or natural disasters and ensure continuity of business by having resilient, diverse communications capability in place. The plans will also identify how to respond to, and recover from, such attacks in a manner that limits the consequences and value of such attacks. In addition, DoD will collaborate with the owner/operators to formulate the most suitable balance of prevention, detection, protection, response, recovery, and resiliency for critical DIB assets using the results of risk assessments.

DoD's goals:

- **Prevent or Delay an Incident**. DoD will collaborate with critical DIB asset owners to jointly determine additional measures needed to prevent or delay an incident beyond those measures that are contractually required.

- **Detect a Potential Incident**. DoD will collaborate with critical asset owners to jointly determine additional measures needed to detect potential incidents beyond those measures that are contractually required. DoD will also support and facilitate sharing of threat information through appropriate government and commercial channels.

- **Mitigate or Respond to an Incident**. DoD will collaborate with critical asset owners to encourage the preparation and exercise of business continuity plans beyond those that are contractually required. DoD and asset owners will review the requirement for sub-tier supplier business continuity planning. As the consumer of DIB products and services, DoD and asset owners will periodically review actions needed to respond to an incident, consistent with the principles of layered defense described previously.

- **Recover From an Incident**. DoD will collaborate with critical asset owners to encourage preparation and exercise of business continuity plans supporting recovery from an incident.

- **Develop Resiliency**. DoD will evaluate the costs and benefits of adding redundancy of DIB capabilities and services, thus reducing the number of critical DIB assets. When working with asset owner/operators, DoD will also explore approaches to improving the resiliency of services, production processes, supply chains, and associated facilities and information systems.

5.2 Determining Protective Program Needs

DoD will collaborate with critical DIB asset owners to examine the cost/benefit associated with additional measures needed to protect critical service and product delivery consistent with DoD policy. DoD and the asset owners will decide which additional measures should be instituted and develop a strategy to distribute costs associated with this effort.

5.3 Protective Program Implementation

Implementation of DIB protection programs relies upon certain core actions and processes that consist of:

- Plans that address remediation of vulnerabilities, mitigation, and consequence management for the facility;

- Development of protective capabilities, commitments, and forces internal or external to the facility;

- Application of the information from the analysis and assessment processes;

- Continual monitoring of adverse changes in threat, environment, criticality, and prior factors of consequence; execution of agreed remediation and mitigation strategies; and the degree of progress and impact at the facility, Federal, State, and local levels, including the information sources and processes;

- Contingency planning and execution;

- Referral and reporting;

- Education, awareness, and training; and

- Processes, tools, and resources to raise the level of preparedness among the critical DIB assets and within the DIB in general.

The critical DIB asset owner is responsible for providing for its protection and security, which is usually accomplished through normal business continuity plans and programs. The criticality notification process conveys the criticality determination, solicits and confirms company and facility agreement to engage in the process, and provides recommendations on immediate and longer term actions. ASD(HD&ASA), working with appropriate DoD offices, will oversee the notification process. DoD will ensure information about criticality determination is shared with the organizations responsible for protecting the asset.

In addition to the protective measures taken by the DIB asset owner/operator, local law enforcement and other first-responders and State resources are available to respond to emergencies. However, protection of critical DIB assets may require additional measures to prevent, deter, and mitigate threats and hazards, and to minimize vulnerabilities.

If, as an outcome of an onsite assessment, DoD identifies an unacceptable level of risk associated with the critical DIB asset, then DoD leadership, in collaboration with the asset owner, will explore one or more of the following actions:

- Conduct remediation activities (e.g., minimize or eliminate vulnerabilities);

- Develop mitigation plans (e.g., execute contingency plans, strengthen security measures);

- Develop response plans (e.g., scenario-specific emergency response);

- Prepare for an infrastructure incident (exercise contingency plans) and integrate into other sector exercise and evaluation programs; and/or

- Develop reconstitution tradeoff analyses (e.g., outline alternative sources of supply).

In addition, DoD or the DIB asset owner may partially or fully employ the following practices to enhance protection of their assets:

- Those who contract for non-DoD-owned infrastructure services and products will negotiate with public and private sector organizations to enhance the security of supporting DIB assets. Critical DIB asset owners and those who contract for non-DoD infrastructure services and products will monitor risk. As potential threats and infrastructures change, reviews of previous risk analyses may be conducted to determine if remediation or mitigation recommendations should be changed.

- DoD expects a facility or company, in addition to its own resources and those with which it contracts, to use local and State law enforcement, and other local and State emergency resources, to meet its emergency needs. State and local law enforcement and other emergency responders also monitor factors under their purview in the local environment. They provide advice, assistance, warning and alert; incorporate the facility into emergency planning; and prioritize it for response and other services.

- DoD policies and procedures ensure prompt and appropriate sharing of critical asset and facility information with FBI headquarters, which may provide further dissemination to FBI field offices and incorporate such information into its planning and operations. The FBI will report to the supporting DoD industrial security and counterintelligence activities any adverse information impacting a DIB facility and, when requested, brief DoD officials and other key partners.

- The FBI may use the Joint Terrorism Task Force structure to help provide reporting and protection for the critical DIB asset, subject to restrictions that DoD may place on dissemination of the asset information.

- The DHS and the Federal Emergency Management Agency (FEMA), in particular, offer emergency assistance that a critical DIB asset may elect to use. DoD will collaborate with DIB owner/operators to evaluate that assistance, and other services those organizations may offer, to better enable informed decisions regarding:

  – How the facility should interface;
  – What information it should provide;
  – What assistance it should seek related to its status as a critical DIB asset; and
  – How DoD should proceed to promote and facilitate such assistance across critical DIB assets.

- SSAs, the DHS, and the national intelligence community will have information directly relevant to critical DIB assets. DoD is collaborating with its partners to ensure full integration and appropriate sharing of information that does, or could, adversely affect an asset's capacity or survivability.

- DoD components will execute their assigned roles as prescribed in DoD policy. DoD will promptly share information regarding the potential endangerment of a critical DIB asset with partners that have protection roles as identified in this plan.

- Combatant commands provide for planning and coordination of military force deployment and protection of designated critical facilities in their geographic areas of responsibility. DoD will develop the procedures for contingency military protection of critical DIB assets, and specify the responsibilities of combatant commanders, military departments, and National Guard forces under Title 10 or Title 32 of United States Code (U.S.C.). Combatant commanders will coordinate all such protection plans/activities relating to DIB assets in foreign countries with the U.S. ambassadors in those countries.

5.4 Protective Program Performance

Protective program performance will be monitored by DoD and the DIB SCC as described in section 6.

6. Measure Progress

6.1 Critical Infrastructure Performance Measurement

This section describes measures used to evaluate risk management progress for the DIB Sector. Measuring progress for the sector has two distinct, yet inter-related, components:

- Core NIPP metrics that measure progress for SSP Implementation developed by the DHS for application to all national sectors; and

- DIB Sector metrics.

Preliminary metrics focus on prescribed core NIPP implementation actions (NIPP appendix 2B) and on DIB Sector goals and objectives for which active engagement with DIB security partners is not completed. DoD expects the metrics to evolve as NIPP and DIB SSP efforts mature.

Table 6-1 describes Core NIPP progress implementation metrics applicable to all sectors.

Table 6-1: Core NIPP Implementation Metrics

Implementation Action	Type of Metric	Metric	Expected Completion Date
Authorities, Roles, and Responsibilities			
Review NIPP and establish processes needed to support implementation.	Descriptive	Milestone	Completed
Incorporate NIPP into strategies for cooperation with foreign countries and international/multinational organizations.	Output	Milestone	March 30, 2007
Protection Program Strategy: Managing Risk			
Develop sector-specific critical infrastructure inventory guidance.	Output	Milestone	Completed
Review existing risk assessment methodologies to determine compatibility with the NIPP baseline.	Process	Milestone	March 30, 2007
Establish timeline for (1) development of sector-specific risk methodologies, and (2) conducting consequence-based top-screening for all critical infrastructure sectors.	Output	Milestone	December 30, 2006
Conduct and validate consequence assessments of priority critical infrastructure as identified by the top-screening process.	Process	Milestone	June 30, 2008
Conduct or facilitate vulnerability assessments in priority critical infrastructure sectors and identify cross-sector vulnerabilities.	Process	Milestone	June 30, 2013

Implementation Action	Type of Metric	Metric	Expected Completion Date
Organizing and Partnering for Critical Infrastructure Protection			
Establish SCC, GCC in accordance with the NIPP partnership model.	Process	Milestone	Completed
Complete rollout of Homeland Security Information Network for Critical Sectors (HSIN-CS) Community of Interest (COI); implement policies for vetting and disseminating information to security partners.	Process	Milestone	June 30, 2007
Identify sector-level, information-sharing mechanisms and ensure that information protection practices comply with appropriate guidance for protection of classified or sensitive information.	Process	Milestone	September 30, 2007
Work with DOS to review the charter and coordinating mechanisms for the interagency working group that coordinates U.S. international CIP outreach and update as needed to align with the NIPP.	Process	Milestone	March 30, 2007
Integrating Critical Infrastructure Protection as Part of the Homeland Security Program			
Coordinate SSP development in collaboration with security partners and submit to the DHS with appropriate documentation of concurrence.	Process	Milestone	December 30, 2006
Review and revise critical infrastructure-related plans as needed to reinforce linkage between NIPP steady-state CIP and National Response Plan (NRP) incident management requirements.	Process	Milestone	March 30, 2007
Review current CIP measures to ensure alignment with Homeland Security Advisory System threat conditions and specific threat vectors/scenarios.	Process	Milestone	March 30, 2007
Ensuring Effective, Efficient Program Over the Long Term			
Develop and implement a comprehensive National Critical Infrastructure Protection Awareness Program.	Process	Milestone	March 30, 2007
Review and, as appropriate, revise training programs to ensure consistency with the NIPP requirements.	Process	Milestone	September 30, 2007
Provide initial NIPP training to security partners.	Process	Milestone	Completed
Ensure that national exercises include critical infrastructure protection and interaction between the NIPP and NRP.	Process	Milestone	Completed
Communicate requirements for critical infrastructure-related R&D to the DHS for use in the national R&D planning effort.	Output	Milestone	July 1, annually
Identify all databases, data services and sources, and modeling capabilities with critical infrastructure applications.	Process	Milestone	June 30, 2007
Conduct first annual review of the NIPP and SSP.	Process	Milestone	June 30, 2007
Providing Resources of the Critical Infrastructure Protection Program			
Submit sector CIP annual report to the DHS.	Output	Milestone	July 1, annually
Advise State, local, and tribal governments of SSA grant programs to address critical infrastructure grants and/or other sources that can support the NIPP.	Output	Milestone	March 30, 2007

6.1.1 Developing Sector-Specific Metrics

OASD(HD&ASA) and the DIB SCC are responsible for collaboratively developing DIB sector-specific metrics to track SSP implementation progress. DoD, as the SSA, records and reports DIB sector-specific metrics to the DHS on behalf of DoD, SCC, and the DIB.

The process of developing the metrics begins with strategic planning subject matter experts drafting metrics that correspond to DIB Sector security goals and the type of metrics in the SSP Guidance. This SSP emphasizes output and outcome metrics, but also includes descriptive and process metrics. These metrics will evolve as the DoD-SCC partnership and common perspective of plans and expectations mature. DoD and the DIB SCC will review and approve the metrics jointly, and will continue to monitor the metrics during annual comprehensive program reviews.

Table 6-2 presents an unvetted, preliminary set of metrics for each security goal.

Table 6-2: DIB Sector-Specific Goals and Metrics

Description	Type of Metric	Metric
Goal 1: Critical Asset Reduction		
Objective A: DoD will strive to reduce the number of critical DIB assets whenever and wherever possible within fiscal and legal constraints. Sector resiliency would be most assured if no particular asset could be assessed as more critical than any other; the ultimate goal would be zero critical DIB assets.	Output	Number of Critical DIB Assets
Objective B: Share and advance sound risk management practices, including infrastructure asset resiliency, mitigation of risks, and redundancy throughout the DIB.	Outcome	Results of Solicited DIB Asset Owner Feedback
Goal 2: Personnel Security		
Goal: Ensure all personnel associated directly with a critical DIB asset are vetted for employment suitability, reliability, and trustworthiness using established processes commensurate with requirements of the positions held and in conformance with pertinent security policy.	Outcome	DIB Asset Owner Reporting
Objective A: Using the current profile of critical DIB assets, no later than the second quarter of each fiscal year, determine the fiscal-year vetting requirement and associated costs to fully achieve the stated goal above; solicit the cooperation of DoD acquisition and procurement officials, and critical DIB asset (owner/operators); determine the contract implications of findings.	Process Outcome	Completed Statements of Vetting Requirements No Negative Findings
Objective B: Survey critical DIB asset owner/operators for their respective current practices to determine characteristics of the personnel security requirements, particularly for contracts involving no classified information.	Output	Proportion of DIB Asset Owners Reporting
Goal 3: Physical Security		
Goal: Determine the impact or consequence of critical DIB facility loss to the DoD mission(s) supported, the known or perceived threat, and the vulnerability; identify specific DIB assets the destruction or disruption of which could result in human casualties or economic disruption similar to the effects of weapons of mass destruction; compile a composite of facility physical security risk assessments.	Output	Number of Completed DIB Critical Facility Physical Security Risk Assessments
Objective A: Conduct or facilitate physical security assessments for the moderate to high-risk critical DIB assets based on the prevailing threat environment.	Process	Number of Annual High-Consequence Assessments Completed
Objective B: Compile for each fiscal year an appropriately redacted summary report of physical security assessments from Objective A above, for the security officers responsible for critical DIB assets, and for DoD program, acquisition, procurement, and financial officials with oversight of the critical DIB asset.	Output	Completed Timely Report

Description	Type of Metric	Metric
Goal 4: Information Security		
Goal: All information that identifies or otherwise describes characteristics of a critical DIB asset that is created, held, and maintained by the government or the private sector will be protected from unauthorized disclosure according to established procedures appropriate to the particular level of information.	Outcome	Reports of Disclosures and Compliance
Objective A: Protect from unauthorized disclosure, according to established procedures appropriate to the particular level of information, other operations security considerations, or specific contract provisions, all information that identifies or otherwise describes characteristics of a critical DIB asset that is created, held, and maintained by the government or the private sector, whichever is most appropriate.	Outcome	Number of Unauthorized Disclosures
Objective B: Implement appropriate policy provisions to protect sensitive technology.	Outcome	Proportion of Private Sector DIB Asset Owners in Compliance
Goal 5: Information Assurance		
Goal: DIB asset owners will have functional and adequate plans in place for exercising prudent information assurance methods to protect the critical DIB asset, control processes over the production or provisioning of the critical product or service, and the product or service delivery systems, including the supply chain.	Outcome	Proportion of DIB Asset Owners Capable of Demonstrating Effectiveness of IA Based on Exercised Plans
Goal 6: Insider Threat		
Goal: DoD will provide security education and training aids to critical DIB asset owner/operators that do not have security programs so that they may implement provisions for vetting system and network administrators commensurate with the consequence of loss of sensitive or classified information, production or provisioning capability, and supply chain integrity.	Outcome	Validated Information Systems Integrity
Goal 7: Monitoring and Reporting		
Goal: Determine the effectiveness of government threat reporting to officials, owners, and operators responsible for critical DIB assets, and local law enforcement officials and other first-responders including, as appropriate, the local medical and mass transportation communities.	Process	Results of Solicited DIB Asset Owner Feedback
Goal 8: Training and Education		
Goal: Develop specific security education and training materials for critical DIB asset owner/operators.	Outcome	Proportion of DIB Asset Owners Implementing Security Education and Training Materials

At every meeting, DoD and the DIB SCC will review the outcome metrics to determine the extent to which the DIB security partners are achieving the intended sector outcome for protection of critical DIB assets as well as the identified potential points of failure supporting other sector critical infrastructure.

Table 6-3, in section 6.2, describes unvetted, preliminary DIB SSP milestones aligned with the NIPP risk management framework, in addition to stating the implementation action and authorities responsible for completing the action.

6.1.2 Information Collection and Verification

OASD(HD&ASA), in collaboration with the DIB SCC, will assess and verify progress data for core and DIB sector-specific metrics. Facilitated by the DIB SCC membership, DoD will compile the data from the DIB owner/operators.

The DIB SCC will approve all data calls prior to issuance. DoD will request at least one data call annually to support preparation of the annual report to the DHS until a controlled-access, Web-enabled server is deployed to support reporting needs. When the Web-enabled capability is operational, DIB asset owner/operators and other security partners will be able to post and query data as needed. DoD and the DIB SCC will determine access authorities jointly to help protect sensitive data.

DoD and the DIB SCC will assess annually, beginning in July 2007, the effectiveness of metrics; the progress of goals, objectives, and actions they measure; DIB owner/operator data submissions; and will monitor postings of DIB owner/operator-provided data on a DoD Web-enabled collection site, when available. DoD will monitor contract performance for those contracts with provisions that contribute to DIB sector-specific security goals.

DoD and the DIB SCC will jointly determine, prior to collecting data for the annual report, whether it is necessary to collect and/or include sensitive or proprietary data to satisfy the requirement to report progress against the core and sector-specific metrics.

6.1.3 Reporting

In accordance with NIPP sections 3.6.3 (Assessing Performance and Reporting on Progress) and 7.1.1 (Sector-Specific Agency Reporting to the DHS), and section 8 (Managing and Coordinating SSA Responsibilities), the DIB Sector annual report will:

- Include a baseline description of existing sector-specific critical asset protection programs and initiatives;

- Describe DoD SSA resource requirements and available DIB critical infrastructure protection budget;

- Describe or update the description of how DIB Sector efforts (protection programs and initiatives) support the national effort;

- Provide an overall progress report for the sector in comparison to the national CIP goals for the DIB; and

- Describe best practices learned from successful DIB Sector programs and initiatives.

DoD will provide updated measurement and metrics data to the DHS periodically to support DHS status report production. DoD will report DIB Sector progress to the DHS in a format that addresses the requirements of this section or as requested by the DHS. In addition, DoD will describe whether and how the DIB Sector progress metrics support compliance reporting requirements with other statutes or regulations.

DoD will treat and appropriately mark DIB Sector metrics and progress data in accordance with the DoD CIP Classification Guide and other information-handling rules such as Protected Critical Infrastructure Information (PCII). DoD will share the metrics and progress report with the DIB SCC and with the DHS to support the latter's monitoring of national sectors defined in HSPD-7.

6.2 Implementation Actions

This section describes DIB sector-specific implementation actions. DoD and the DIB SCC have identified numerous implementation actions and milestones that they agree to pursue according to the requirements of the action. Table 6-3 lists unvetted, preliminary DIB Sector implementation actions, action milestones, and organizational implementing agents. It also lists corresponding NIPP risk management framework stages.

Table 6-3: DIB Sector Implementation Actions

NIPP Risk Management Framework Stage	DIB SSP Implementation Action	Milestone(s)	Implementation Agent
Initial NIPP Implementation Initiatives and Actions	Establish a DIB Government Coordinating Council (GCC).	Completed	ASD(HD&ASA)/CIP Directorate
	Convene a meeting of DIB industry associations to draft a DIB SCC charter.	Completed	National Defense Industrial Association
	Establish DIB SCC Charter, select a chairperson.	Completed	SCC
	Convene periodic GCC and SCC meetings; convene joint GCC-SCC meeting at least once annually.	Quarterly and as needed	DIB GCC and SCC chairpersons
	Complete enrollment in HSIN-CS COI.	Completed	DIB owner/operators
	Implement policies for vetting and disseminating information to security partners.	June 30, 2007	DIB SCC
Set Security Goals	Develop and coordinate a DoD Defense Sector Assurance Plan.	December 30, 2006	Defense Contract Management Agency
	Draft and vet DIB Sector security goals and metrics with DIB GCC and SCC.	December 30, 2006	ASD(HD&ASA)/CIP Directorate
	Evaluate effectiveness of goals; adjust targets as necessary.	July 1, annually	ASD(HD&ASA)/CIP Directorate and NDIA
Identify Assets, Systems, Networks, and Functions	Collaborate with other SSAs to identify cross-sector interdependencies.	July 1, annually	GCC and SCC
Assess Risks	Adapt mission assurance model to assess risks for DIB impact on public health and safety, governance, economic, public confidence, and national security, in addition to national defense.	June 30, 2007	USD(AT&L) with support of DCMA
	Report risk assessments to the DIB GCC and SCC.	July 1, annually	ASD(HD&ASA)/CIP Directorate
	Implement common direction and guidance from the DIB GCC and SCC.	Within 60 days of notification	ASD(HD&ASA)/CIP Directorate
Prioritize	Prioritize critical DIB assets in accordance with NIPP criteria.	July 1, annually	ASD(HD&ASA)/CIP Directorate supported by DCMA

NIPP Risk Management Framework Stage	DIB SSP Implementation Action	Milestone(s)	Implementation Agent
Implement Protective Programs (Personnel Security)	Personnel Security – Issue first data call to all DIB human resources offices to confirm use of employment suitability checks for employees associated directly with a critical DIB asset in unclassified information environments.	150 days after issuance, then annually	DIB GCC and SCC, jointly
	Personnel Security Objective A – Assess DIB human resources office responses (requirements and associated costs, including costs to respond) to the above data call and determine the contract implications of findings.	September 1, 2007	DIB GCC and SCC, jointly
	Personnel Security Objective B: Evaluate survey of DIB human resources offices responsible for critical DIB assets for contracts involving no classified information.	60 days after issuance of SSP	GCC
Implement Protective Programs (Physical Security)	Physical Security: Complete identification of critical DIB assets based on HSPD-7 criteria.	September 1, 2007, then annually	GCC
	Physical Security Objective A: Complete security assessments on high-risk critical DIB assets determined by the prevailing threat environment issued by the DHS.	Annually or as required	GCC
	Physical Security Objective B: Prepare and submit physical security assessments report to the DHS.	July 1, annually	ASD(HD&ASA)/CIP Directorate
	Information Security Objective: Evaluate effectiveness of compliance with appropriate information security policies.	July 1, annually	USD(I) and USD(AT&L) in collaboration with ASD(HD&ASA)
	Information Assurance: Evaluate effectiveness of individual and collective critical DIB asset owner information assurance programs based on completed exercises of those plans.	July 1, annually	ASD (NII) in collaboration with ASD(HD&ASA)
	Insider Threat: Evaluate effectiveness of individual critical DIB asset owner efforts to deter the insider threat.	July 1, annually	USD(I), ASD(NII) in collaboration with ASD(HD&ASA)
	Monitoring and Reporting: Evaluate effectiveness of DoD and the DHS efforts to provide timely and effective threat and hazard warnings to critical DIB asset owners.	July 1, annually	DIB GCC and SCC

NIPP Risk Management Framework Stage	DIB SSP Implementation Action	Milestone(s)	Implementation Agent
Implement Protective Programs (Training and Education)	Training and Education: Evaluate feedback from critical DIB asset owners regarding the effectiveness of training materials.	July 1, annually	USD(AT&L) with support of DCMA, USD(I), and the SCC
	Critical Asset Reduction Objective A: Prepare and submit report to the DIB GCC and SCC on the current and projected number of critical DIB assets.	March 1, annually	USD(AT&L) with support of DCMA
	Critical Asset Reduction Objective B: Solicit feedback from critical DIB asset owners on the effectiveness and advances in infrastructure risk management practices.	July 1, annually	USD(AT&L) with support of DCMA and the SCC
Measure Effectiveness	Review assessment of DIB Sector metrics.	July 1, annually	DIB GCC and SCC
Other DIB Sector Actions	Identify and compile recommendations on the best approaches to enhancing security and protecting infrastructures critical to DoD based on canvassing DoD components and the DIB SCC.	July 1, annually	ASD(HD&ASA)/CIP Directorate
	Sponsor DIB GCC/SCC conferences to identify and discuss common CIP issues.	May 1, then periodically based on demand	ASD(HD&ASA) partnering with NDIA
	Refine and promote roles and responsibilities for working with industry regarding DCIP DIB, building on existing relationships between government and industry, and using MOUs to formalize relationships.	Continuing	DIB GCC and SCC supported by ASD(HD&ASA) CIP Directorate
	Develop operational relationships with other Federal departments and agencies (e.g., the DHS, TSA, USCG, FBI, DOS, DOC, and OSTP) to ensure the DCIP DIB risk management strategy is consistent with, and fully supports, the DoD critical infrastructure risk management strategy and national CIP efforts, including those efforts that address cyber risks.	Continuing	ASD(HD&ASA)/CIP Directorate supported by the DIB GCC and SCC

6.3 Challenges and Continuous Improvement

DoD and the DIB SCC will collaborate to develop DIB sector-specific metrics to track SSP implementation progress. DoD, as the SSA, will record and report the metrics to the DHS. The metrics will be monitored via annual comprehensive program reviews for efficacy and to assess progress toward meeting accepted goals.

A significant challenge will be acceptance of the NIPP and SSP by the DIB at large. DoD will work diligently and in a collaborative manner with all security partners to garner support for the goals, objectives, and metrics in the SSP.

Where DIB assets are located in foreign countries, many of the plan's proposed activities could be perceived as U.S. government intrusion into sovereign areas of the host country, particularly with respect to reports on threats and vulnerabilities. DoD and the DIB SSC must ensure that DIB protection activities are coordinated with U.S. embassies and host governments. Where pertinent treaties or agreements exist, activities should conform to them. The DIB SSC should work with DOS to develop a strategy for promulgating this action plan in foreign countries with DIB assets.

At least yearly, DoD and the DIB SCC will review the outcome metrics to assess the extent to which DIB security partners are achieving the intended sector outcome for protection of critical DIB assets as well as the identified potential points of failure supporting other sector-critical infrastructures.

7. CI/KR Protection Research and Development

7.1 Overview of Sector R&D

HSPD-7 establishes an annual requirement for the National Critical Infrastructure Protection Research and Development Plan (NCIP R&D Plan). As the primary R&D organization of the DHS, the Science and Technology Directorate (S&T) prepares the annual NCIP R&D Plan in partnership with OSTP. The long-term vision of the NCIP R&D Plan is set out in three strategic goals:

- A national common operating picture for critical infrastructures;

- A next-generation Internet architecture with security "designed in" and inherent in all elements rather than added after the fact; and

- Resilient, self-diagnosing, and self-healing physical and cyber infrastructure systems.

HSPD-7 also instructs OSTP and the DHS to coordinate interagency R&D to enhance protection of CI/KR. Sectors must collaborate on the plan to properly identify and reduce redundant efforts at R&D solutions. To assist the agencies and sector industries in coordinating their R&D, the DHS S&T and OSTP have organized the NCIP R&D Plan into nine research theme areas:

- Detection and Sensor Systems;

- Protection;

- Entry Portals;

- Insider Threats;

- Analysis and Decision Support Methods;

- Response, Recovery, and Reconstitution;

- New and Emerging Threats and Vulnerabilities;

- Advanced Infrastructure Architectures and System Designs; and

- Human/Social Issues.

Each theme area includes both physical and cyber R&D, and each supports the three NCIP R&D strategic goals. The 2004 NCIP R&D Plan is available at: www.dhs.gov/interweb/assetlibrary/ST_2004_NCIP_RD_PlanFINALApr05.pdf.

DoD supports OSTP and the DHS S&T in developing the NCIP R&D Plan. As the SSA, DoD recognizes the need to develop, manage, and coordinate R&D requirements and activities for the DIB Sector. These requirements and activities should complement and leverage ongoing DoD R&D, addressing the CIP needs of DoD and its DIB security partners. DoD input to the plan will consist of a list of all R&D activities related to CIP for the DIB Sector coordinated with industry security partners through the DIB SSC.

7.2 Sector R&D Requirements

DoD will work with its DIB security partners to identify the DIB Sector capability requirements supportable through technology development. DoD will analyze the requirements to identify potential R&D initiatives. Once R&D requirements are identified, they will be analyzed to determine which existing programs can be leveraged and which new programs should be fostered.

DoD will maintain a list of DIB Sector technology requirements and will evaluate them annually against the DHS S&T- and OSTP-correlated input. DoD, in coordination with the DIB GCC and SCC, will identify gaps between the DIB requirements and the current R&D initiatives to ensure the continuity and priority of sector R&D efforts.

7.3 Sector R&D Plan

DoD has launched a number of initiatives already and is currently in the process of developing a unified R&D plan to better coordinate ongoing and planned efforts. DoD will coordinate with the DIB GCC and SCC as the plan evolves. Additional activities will focus on:

- A criticality methodology and prioritization process that will enable resources to be focused on higher risk assets;
- A Web-based self-assessment process that addresses asset criticality and vulnerability as well as risk mitigation and consequence remediation preparation;
- Onsite assessments based upon asset criticality and vulnerability findings;
- A process for followup on vulnerability assessments' action items;
- Consolidating information from the various processes and activities within DoD, other Federal departments and agencies, and sources such as State and local authorities, and ensuring a process exists for dissemination of information to stakeholders;
- Analysis of available information from the assessment process (and other sources) and development of a risk management report, with recommendations, guidance, and direction;
- Consequence management reports, including recommendations, potential impacts, cost estimates, and schedules;
- Interdiction by various levels as determined by risk (imminence and magnitude):
  - DIB owner/operator self-review/reporting;
  - State or local authorities; and
  - DoD or other Federal departments and agencies; and
- Development and distribution of a process for developing Mission Assurance Plans.

DoD and DND-Canada entered into an agreement whereby they can more efficiently continue their efforts to improve the defense posture of the North American technology and industrial base. The NATIBO is chartered to promote a cost-effective, healthy technology and industrial base that is responsive to the national and economic security needs of the United States and Canada. Current policy calls for a national defense force that derives its strength and technical superiority from a unified commercial/military industrial base. Outlined in a bilateral MOU, dated May 30, 2001, the policy objectives are to:

- Effectively leverage dollars/resources and reduce redundant efforts through bilateral cooperation on studies and projects relating to the defense technology and industrial base of the United States and Canada;
- Achieve rapid technology insertion and commercialization of emerging technologies that can be used in the manufacture and repair of defense materiel; and

- Permit a wide variety of work to be accomplished on a single project, from paper studies and initial research to technology insertion efforts.

The DIB security partners will continue to monitor and encourage the NATIBO process to ensure an adequate industrial technology base.

The NATIBO US/CA Homeland Defense (HD) Working Group will monitor the respective initiatives and projects of the U.S. DoD/HD and Canadian DND, identify potential HD-related cooperative R&D projects, and conduct bilateral HD-related studies and projects under the NATIBO MOU. DoD anticipates future cooperative research, development, test, and evaluation projects between DoD and DND-Canada.

7.4 R&D Management Process

DoD will leverage the DHS R&D efforts and national technologies and share those approaches with the DIB asset owner/operators and other security partners as appropriate. DoD will identify technology requirements in support of the DIB annually through an evaluation of the challenges reported in this document, analysis of the requirements needed to support initiatives identified in this document, and evaluation of the technologies DoD needs to support the required DIB metrics. DoD will gather further requirements in support of the DIB through data calls among the security partners.

DoD will annually solicit a listing of current CIP R&D initiatives from OSTP to evaluate for potential support of DIB requirements. DoD will take its annual integrated list of technology requirements in support of the DIB and group this list in categories related to the themes of the NCIP R&D Plan. DoD will then request that the DHS S&T and OSTP correlate their categorized list of requirements with the NCIP R&D list of current initiatives. The DHS S&T and OSTP will then provide the relevant initiatives back to DoD.

Upon receipt of the correlated list of NCIP R&D initiatives and DIB requirements from the DHS S&T and OSTP, DoD will conduct working sessions to evaluate the most feasible initiatives to support the DIB requirements. Upon evaluation and validation of potential initiatives, DoD will forward its recommendations to the directorate and OSTP.

8. Managing and Coordinating SSA Responsibilities

DoD's legacy CIP program took a centralized management and coordination approach to meet DoD's security goals and Presidential Decision Directive 63 responsibilities. Those program goals focused on DoD mission assurance. With issuance of HSPD-7, however, DoD is shifting to a decentralized management approach for mission continuity and expanding responsibilities as the DIB SSA to include consideration of the impact to other national security concerns.

8.1 Program Management Approach

DoD's program management approach focuses on the SSA responsibilities assigned in HSPD-7 to:

- Collaborate with all relevant Federal departments and agencies, State and local governments, and the private sector, including key people and entities in their infrastructure sectors;

- Conduct or facilitate vulnerability assessments of the DIB Sector; and

- Encourage risk management strategies to protect against and mitigate the effects of attacks against CI/KR.

To execute DIB SSA responsibilities, DoD seeks to engage in ongoing activities that:

- Improve trust between the government and DIB owner/operators to support two-way information sharing;

- Maintain meaningful and frequent dialogue across the diverse array of DIB security partners; and

- Ameliorate the burden for remediating or mitigating vulnerabilities for the highest priority critical DIB assets wherever possible.

DoD is collaborating with its security partners through the DIB GCC and SCC to manage program priorities and respond to industry needs.

8.2 Processes and Responsibilities

8.2.1 SSP Maintenance and Update

DoD will initiate an annual security partner review of the SSP. If revisions are significant, the plan will be updated and reissued consistent with DHS guidance. DoD considers the members of the DIB GCC and SCC to be full partners in preparing and executing the DIB SSP. Each member will provide an acknowledgement letter regarding its participation in developing and maintaining the plan.

8.2.2 Annual Reporting

DoD collaborates with its sector security partners to acquire the information necessary to prepare the DIB Sector annual report. As operational lead, DCMA works with the DIB GCC and SCC to establish effective information collection mechanisms. DCMA, supported by the DIB SCC where applicable and in conformance with its charter, will collect information from owners, operators, and suppliers.

8.2.3 Resources and Budgets

To date, DoD has maintained centralized responsibility for building, managing, and tracking the DIB CIP program budget and resources at DoD headquarters level. Currently, however, DCMA is beginning to share in the process.

DoD has used a strategic and performance management model to meet both DoD internal agency CIP and SSA responsibilities. DoD will review the mission and vision statements, guiding principles, and organizational values annually and refine and prioritize the goals presented in section 1. DoD builds funding plans to support capabilities required to perform activities and then uses outcome-based metrics to track performance.

In the near term, DoD will continue to manage the policy, oversight, and advocacy elements of the budget, and DCMA will manage the integration and coordination elements to execute the responsibilities. The DIB GCC and SCC will contribute to the development of sector requirements and priorities for CIP to inform the resource management process.

8.2.4 Training and Education

DoD understands that a successful DIB risk management effort requires effective training, education, and outreach. DoD seeks to expand those efforts and support DIB Sector security partners in expanding their education and training. To communicate the importance of these efforts effectively, DoD will meet with senior executives and managers, intelligence analysts, assessment teams, and security personnel. Current training, education, and outreach programs include:

DCIP Awareness Visits: DoD organizes awareness visits to include representatives from the full spectrum of DIB security partners, including the asset owner/operators, the National Guard Bureau, the DHS, the FBI, State and local governments, local responders, and law enforcement officials. The intent of the DCIP awareness visit is to educate the audience, particularly facility security and management personnel and local first-responders, regarding the DoD CIP responsibilities and goals. This is designed to:

- Increase the awareness level of DIB owners, managers, security personnel, and local first-responders regarding potential threats to ongoing business operations;

- Establish or strengthen relationships and foster collaboration between DIB owner/operators and local first-responders, inform local security partners of the importance of these facilities, and support planning for risk mitigation and incident management at these facilities; and

- Ascertain whether facilities have taken any steps to reduce the threat to their facility or to business continuity in the event of an incident.

DIB Mission Assurance Assessment Training: This training is provided by the West Virginia National Guard Training Center and is intended for individuals who perform assessments. The training center offers 2 weeks of training broken out in three levels:

- Overview of the DIB asset prioritization and risk management process with enough detail to communicate what is required to protect infrastructure;

- Concepts and elements of the assessment process; and

- Specific assessment techniques.

DIB Annual Training Conference: DoD sponsors a conference to bring together DoD senior officials with DoD leaders and analysts to enhance DIB capabilities. The conference includes a series of presentations delivered by DoD leaders, private sector representatives and international partners. In addition, a series of technical breakout working sessions are accomplished.

Level I Anti-Terrorism Awareness: The objective is to train individuals on the indicators of terrorism and how to properly report their findings.

Computer Security Awareness: This type of training is available to all levels of DoD employees. DoD deals every day with sensitive information involving payment of billions of dollars each year to industry, matters that could involve the safety and security of our Nation's war fighters and private sector business-sensitive and proprietary information. Emphasis is on handling and safeguarding this type of information and the importance of computer security.

DIB Technology Exhibition: In 2007, NDIA will partner with DoD to sponsor a DIB CIP Symposium and Technology Exhibition. This event is designed to enhance public and private sector collaboration and mutual understanding of the roles of municipal and State governments and agencies, the Federal Government, and industry in building a resilient DIB. The event will emphasize the importance of building and maintaining sufficiently resilient critical infrastructure and supply chains that will defeat terrorist attempts to disrupt our Nation.

8.3 Implementing the Sector Partnership Model

8.3.1 NIPP Coordination Councils

The principal coordinating bodies for the DIB are the DIB GCC and SCC. These bodies act as representatives to the Government Cross-Sector Council and Private Sector Cross-Sector Council, respectively, for the DIB and serve as the DIB leadership connection to the NIPP Leadership Council.

DIB Sector GCC

The GCC seeks to provide effective coordination of DIB Sector security strategies and activities, policy, and communication across and within the government and DIB security partners to support the Nation's homeland security mission. In addition, the GCC coordinates with the other infrastructure sectors that interact with the DIB.

The GCC will:

- Identify items for government-wide coordination and communication;

- Identify needs/gaps in plans, programs, policies, procedures, and strategies;

- Acknowledge and recognize successful programs and practices; and

- Leverage complementary resources within government and between government and industry.

The GCC meets at least biannually and will facilitate the sharing of experiences, ideas, best practices, and innovative approaches related to CIP.

GCC members include representatives of the following offices:

- DoD:

  - Assistant Secretary of Defense for Homeland Defense & Americas' Security Affairs – Chairperson;

  - Deputy Under Secretary of Defense for Industrial Policy (OUSD(AT&L));

  - Deputy Chief Information Officer (OASD(NII));

- Chief, National Guard Bureau;

  – Deputy Director, Defense Research & Engineering (OUSD(AT&L));

  – Director, Defense Procurement & Acquisition Policy (OUSD(AT&L));

  – Deputy Under Secretary of Defense for Counterintelligence & Security (OUSD(I)); and

  – Deputy Under Secretary of Defense for Personnel and Readiness (P&R),

- Interagency Partners:

  – DHS Assistant Secretary for Infrastructure Protection (IP);

  – DHS National Communications System;

  – Department of Energy;

  – Department of Transportation;

  – Department of Commerce;

  – Treasury Department;

  – Department of State;

  – Department of Justice, Assistant Attorney General;

  – Department of Health and Human Services;

  – Environmental Protection Agency; and

  – Transportation Security Administration.

The GCC establishes workgroups when substantial investigation, research, or other tasks are required that cannot be achieved at a regular GCC session. Work group reports advise council members on issues, directions, and processes of note.

DIB SCC

The DIB SCC is chartered to enable private sector owner/operators to interact with the DHS, DoD, other SSAs, and among themselves on CIP matters including response and recovery matters. The DIB SCC is a broadly representative, independent, self-governed body organized by DIB owner/operators. While this council is independent of government, it provides the Critical Infrastructure Partnership Advisory Council (CIPAC) the ability to draw as representational a membership as possible from the DIB security partners. The SCC provides a point of contact for internal coordination on a wide range of sector-specific infrastructure protection activities and issues. It further provides a recurring forum for the DIB owner/operators to facilitate information sharing, identify common areas of interest, synergistically leverage activities, illuminate duplicative processes, and develop a prioritized list of required DIB CIP program improvements. Council membership is available to members of any existing industry association predominantly representing significant DIB business interests. Members possess an authoritative knowledge of DIB capabilities and security requirements. The SCC meets at least quarterly. Industry associations participating in the SCC include:

- Aerospace Industries Association (AIA);

- American Society for Industrial Security (ASIS) International;

- Industrial Security Working Group (ISWG);

- National Classification Management Society (NCMS); and

- National Defense Industrial Association (NDIA).

CIPAC provides the opportunity for industry and government partners to discuss DIB-related CIP issues, normally in the form of the GCC and the SCC meeting together. The CIPAC was established by the DHS as a Federal Advisory Committee Act-exempt body. Under this umbrella, DIB security partners may engage in a broad range of activities, such as:

- Planning, coordination, implementation, and operational issues;

- Implementation of security programs;

- Operational activities related to infrastructure protection, including incident response, recovery, and reconstitution; and

- Development and support of national plans, including the NIPP and SSPs.

DOS coordinates the Overseas Security Advisory Council (OSAC) that provides security information to, and coordinates security issues with U.S. businesses overseas. To reduce duplication of effort and enhance the effectiveness of the DHS's CIPAC, DOS's OSAC, and DoD programs for DIB protection in the international arena, the three departments will coordinate their efforts.

Homeland Infrastructure Foundation-Level Database Working Group

The Homeland Infrastructure Foundation-Level Database (HIFLD) Working Group is a coalition of Federal, State, and local government organizations, federally funded R&D centers, and supporting private industry partners. Members are involved with geospatial or "location awareness" issues related to homeland security, homeland defense, civil support, or emergency preparedness and response. Sponsored by OASD(HD&ASA), the HIFLD Working Group includes representatives from numerous government agencies, including the U.S. Northern Command, National Geospatial-Intelligence Agency (NGA), and U.S. Geological Survey (USGS). The group promotes domestic and international infrastructure geospatial information sharing, protection, and knowledge management.

8.3.2 State, Local, and Tribal Government Entities

The DIB SCC and GCC will bring together diverse Federal, State, and local government interests to identify and develop collaborative strategies that advance CIP. Membership in the GCC will include influential leaders on DIB security issues from Federal, State, and local governments. The SCC is considering establishment of a subcouncil for Federal, Regional, State, and Local Response Integration.

8.3.3 International Security Partners

In foreign countries, DoD works through DOS via treaties, Status of Forces Agreements, bilateral agreements, and other available diplomatic tools. Where possible, DoD will include consideration of DIB assets located in areas not under direct U.S. control within the context of these constructs. DoD is involved in CFIUS reviews with other Federal departments and agencies where critical DIB asset security could be impacted adversely by foreign ownership.

In addition, the importance to U.S. national security in general, and the DIB in particular, of controlling the transfer of technology with significant military or intelligence applicability must be emphasized, as well as the need to encourage other nations to implement stringent controls on such technology transfer.

DCMA, the DoD agency responsible for executing the DIB SSA responsibilities, has approximately 10,000 employees in more than 900 locations worldwide. It has an office dedicated to international operations. This capability supports the assessment and risk response aspects of the DIB CIP risk management program. This results in a global DIB CIP effort wherein international critical DIB assets are defined and prioritized, vulnerability assessments are planned, and incident response capabilities are in place to assess the impact of actual events.

DCMA, in conjunction with OASD(HD&ASA), works closely with NATIBO to ensure a cost-effective, healthy technology and industrial base that is responsive to the national and economic security needs of the United States and Canada.

OASD(HD&ASA) and DCMA are working closely with their DND-Canada counterparts to develop and implement a common approach to CIP and cross-border incident response. This SPP effort is developing and implementing compatible protective and response strategies and programs for shared DIB critical infrastructure.

8.4 Information Sharing and Reporting

Many organizations have an interest or role in identifying and coordinating protection of critical DIB assets. Each organization must clearly understand its individual role, as well as the roles of other contributing organizations, to ensure that there are no gaps in response and there is minimal duplication of effort. Also, DoD must ensure each organization is furnished with the information necessary to appropriately prevent, plan for, and respond to incidents.

DoD has identified the venues and mechanisms for sharing information with the various DIB CIP communities of interest. These communities include domestic organizations (including industry); international private industry; international coalitions and allies; Federal, State, and local governments and agencies; and other DoD organizations to identify and coordinate protection of critical DIB assets.

The venues DoD employs to share information include:

* DIB GCC, SCC, and CIPAC meetings;

* DCIP Awareness Visits;

* Industry association meetings and expositions;

* Academic symposia and conferences;

* Electronic and traditional mail; and

* World Wide Web and restricted network portals.

The mechanisms for communicating roles, responsibilities, and concepts for effective DIB CIP efforts include:

* Published policy, directives, instructions, guidance, and methodology;

* Documented concept of operations;

* Presentations and speaking engagements at association, international, Federal, State, and local events, expositions, and conferences;

* Onsite awareness presentations at DIB sites;

* Participation in exercises and published lessons learned; and

* Curricula at Defense and other schools.

The most significant challenge to working with DIB asset owners is establishment of legal provisions to support protection of sensitive, including proprietary, information. The DHS issued the Final Rule on Procedures for Handling Critical Infrastructure Information on September 1, 2006. This rule finalizes the procedures for the PCII Program in governing receipt, validation, handling, storage, marking, and use of critical infrastructure information.

Since the preponderance of the critical infrastructure upon which our national security, economy, and public welfare depend is owned and operated by the private sector, the PCII Program was created to encourage the private sector, by providing special protection, to voluntarily share security-related information about this infrastructure. Information submitted, if it satisfies the requirements of the CII Act, is protected from:

- Freedom of Information Act disclosure;

- State and local disclosure laws; and

- Use in civil litigation.

To comply with these procedures, DoD will appoint a PCII Officer to carry out the responsibilities of:

- Overseeing the handling, use, and storage of PCII;

- Ensuring secure sharing of PCII with appropriate authorities and individuals as set forth in 6 CFR 29.1(a);

- Establishing an ongoing self-inspection program, including periodic review and assessment of compliance in the handling, use, and storage of PCII;

- Establishing additional procedures, measures, and penalties as necessary to prevent unauthorized access to PCII; and

- Ensuring prompt and appropriate coordination with the PCII Program Manager regarding any request, challenge, or complaint arising from implementation of PCII regulations.

DoD plans to develop an accreditation plan for obtaining and certifying PCII. Some DCIP DIB information requires security classification. In these instances, DoD will continue to classify information according to applicable regulations and will follow classified networks and systems accreditation processes for information-sharing needs.

In accordance with applicable laws or regulations, OASD(HD&ASA) and DoD components will collaborate with appropriate private sector entities and continue to encourage development of information-sharing and analysis mechanisms. Also, DoD and other HSPD-7 SSAs will collaborate with the private sector and continue to support sector-coordinating mechanisms.

DoD must develop specific information-sharing policy, processes, and procedures to enhance two-way communication between DoD and DIB asset owners. DoD and industry have a number of separate and distinct information sources; however, to date, there has been little interaction between the two. DoD and the asset owners must work to remedy this if there is to be a collaborative effort in protecting the DIB. This was a particular point of emphasis in FY 2006, with establishment of the DIB SCC and GCC with the intent to effectively share DIB CIP information. For instance, DoD and the DIB SCC are evaluating the capability of HSIN-CS as a tool for sharing information both within the DIB Sector, as well as across other sectors.

Appendix 1: List of Acronyms and Abbreviations

AIA	Aerospace Industries Association		DoDD	Department of Defense Directive
APM	Asset Prioritization Model		DOS	Department of State
ASD (HD&ASA)	Assistant Secretary of Defense for Homeland Defense & Americas' Security Affairs		FBI	Federal Bureau of Investigation
			FEMA	Federal Emergency Management Agency
ASD (NII)	Assistant Secretary of Defense for Networks and Information Integration		FOIA	Freedom of Information Act
			GCC	Government Coordinating Council
ASIS	American Society of Industrial Security		GIG	Global Information Grid
BIS	Bureau of Industry and Security		HITRAC	Homeland Infrastructure Threat and Risk Analysis Center
CCATS	CIFA CIP Arrayed Threats System			
CFIUS	Committee on Foreign Investment in the United States		HSIN-CS	Homeland Security Information Network for Critical Sectors
			HSPD	Homeland Security Presidential Directive
CIFA	Counterintelligence Field Activity		IA	Information Assurance
CII	Critical Infrastructure Information		ISWG	Industrial Security Working Group
CI/KR	Critical Infrastructure and Key Resources		IT	Information Technology
CIP	Critical Infrastructure Protection		MOU	Memorandum of Understanding
CIPAC	Critical Infrastructure Partnership Advisory Council		NATIBO	North American Technology Industrial Base Organization
COI	Community of Interest			
DCIP	Defense Critical Infrastructure Program		NCIP	National Critical Infrastructure Protection
DCMA	Defense Contract Management Agency		NCMS	National Classification Management Society
DEPSECDEF	Deputy Secretary of Defense		NDIA	National Defense Industrial Association
DHS	Department of Homeland Security		NIPP	National Infrastructure Protection Plan
DIB	Defense Industrial Base		NMCC	National Military Command Center
DJIOC	Defense Joint Intelligence Operations Center		NMS	National Military Strategy
			NNSA	National Nuclear Security Administration
DND	Department of National Defence of Canada		NRP	National Response Plan
DOC	Department of Commerce		ODNI	Office of the Director of National Intelligence
DoD	Department of Defense			

OIP	Office of Infrastructure Protection (Division of DHS National Protection and Programs Directorate)
PCII	Protection of Critical Infrastructure Information
R&D	Research and Development
S&T	Science and Technology (DHS Directorate)
SCC	Sector Coordinating Council
SECDEF	Secretary of Defense
SPP	Security and Prosperity Partnership of North America
SSA	Sector-Specific Agency
SSP	Sector-Specific Plan
TSA	Transportation Security Administration
USCG	U.S. Coast Guard
USD (AT&L)	Under Secretary of Defense for Acquisition, Technology, and Logistics
USD (I)	Under Secretary of Defense for Intelligence
USD (P&R)	Under Secretary of Defense for Personnel and Readiness
USGS	U.S. Geological Survey

Appendix 2: References

Statutes

6 U.S.C. 101(9): Homeland Security Act of 2002: Critical Infrastructure Information Act, www.fas.org/sgp/crs/RL31762.pdf.

5 U.S.C. 552: The Freedom of Information Act, as amended 2002, www.usdoj.gov/oip/foia_updates/Vol_XVII_4/page2.htm.

Public Law 107-56, Uniting and Strengthening America by Providing Appropriate Tools Required to Intercept and Obstruct Terrorism Act (USA PATRIOT ACT) of 2001, http://frwebgate.access.gpo.gov/cgi-bin/getdoc.cgi?dbname=107_cong_public_laws&docid=f:publ056.107.pdf.

15 U.S.C. App. 2061 et seq., Public Law 81-774, Defense Production Act of 1950, as amended, www.bis.doc.gov/defenseindustrialbaseprograms/OSIES/offsets/dpastatute.html.

42 U.S.C. 5121 et seq., The Robert T. Stafford Disaster Relief and Emergency Assistance Act, as amended, www.dem.dcc.state.nc.us/mitigation/Library/Stafford.pdf.

National Strategies

The National Strategy for Homeland Security, Office of Homeland Security, White House, July 16, 2002, www.whitehouse.gov/homeland/book.

The National Security Strategy of the United States, White House, March 16, 2006, www.whitehouse.gov/nsc/nss/2006/nss2006.pdf.

National Strategy for Physical Protection of Critical Infrastructure and Key Assets, White House, February 2003, www.dhs.gov/xlibrary/assets/Physical_Strategy.pdf.

Homeland Security Presidential Directives

HSPD-7, Critical Infrastructure Identification, Prioritization, and Protection, White House, December 17, 2003, www.whitehouse.gov/news/releases/2003/12/20031217-5.html.

HSPD-8, National Preparedness, White House, December 17, 2003, www.whitehouse.gov/news/releases/2003/12/20031217-6.html.

Executive Plans and Orders

National Infrastructure Protection Plan of 2006, Department of Homeland Security, 2006, www.dhs.gov/xlibrary/assets/NIPP_Plan.pdf.

Executive Order 13228, Establishing the Office of Homeland Security and the Homeland Security Council, White House, October 8, 2001, as amended, www.whitehouse.gov/news/releases/2001/10/20011008-2.html.

Department of Defense Directives and Strategies

DoDD 3020.40, Defense Critical Infrastructure Program (DCIP), August 19, 2005, www.fas.org/irp/doddir/dod/d3020_40.pdf.

DoDD 5144.1, Assistant Secretary of Defense for Networks and Information Integration/DoD Chief Information Officer (ASD(NII)/DoD CIO), May 5, 2005, www.js.pentagon.mil/whs/directives/corres/html/51441.htm.

DoDD 5200.2, DoD Personnel Security Program, April 9, 1999, www.js.pentagon.mil/whs/directives/corres/html/52002.htm.

DoDD 5220.22, National Industrial Security Program, September 27, 2004, www.dtic.mil/whs/directives/corres/html/522022.htm.

The National Defense Strategy of the United States of America, Department of Defense, March 2005, http://stinet.dtic.mil/cgi-bin/GetTRDoc?AD=ADA431214&Location=U2&doc=GetTRDoc.pdf.

The National Military Strategy of the United States of America: A Strategy for Today, A Vision for Tomorrow, Joint Chiefs of Staff, 2004, www.defenselink.mil/news/Mar2005/d20050318nms.pdf.

Strategy for Homeland Defense and Civil Support, Department of Defense, June 2005, www.defenselink.mil/news/Jun2005/d20050630homeland.pdf.

Guidance and Regulation

National Preparedness Guidance, Department of Homeland Security, April 27, 2005, www.ojp.usdoj.gov/odp/docs/NationalPreparednessGuidance.pdf.

Federal Acquisition Regulations (Combination of DoD, General Services Administration, and National Aeronautical and Space Administration, re-issued March 2005, www.acquisition.gov/far.

Defense Federal Acquisition Regulations (Defense Procurement and Acquisition Policy, re-issued 2006), supplement to Federal Acquisition Regulations, www.acq.osd.mil/dpap/dars/dfars/index.htm.

Defense Priorities and Allocations System, 15 C.F.R. Part 700, January 1, 2003, http://frwebgate5.access.gpo.gov/cgi-bin/waisgate.cgi?WAISdocID=98144053091+1+0+0&WAISaction=retrieve.

The National Plan for Research and Development in Support of Critical Infrastructure Protection, The Executive Office of the President, Office of Science and Technology Policy; Department of Homeland Security, Science and Technology Directorate, 2004, www.ornl.gov/sci/oetd/documents/ST_2004_NCIP_RD_PlanFINALApr05.pdf.

Charters

North American Technology and Industrial Base Charter of 1997, www.acq.osd.mil/ott/natibo/charter.html.

Security and Prosperity Partnership of North America, White House, March 23, 2005, www.whitehouse.gov/news/releases/2005/03/20050323-1.html.

www.ingramcontent.com/pod-product-compliance
Lightning Source LLC
Chambersburg PA
CBHW080542290526
45790CB00006B/2521